GW00694441

Christian Comm

Andrew Lockley

CHRISTIAN COMMUNES

SCM PRESS LTD

For my father and mother

334 01927 3

First published 1976
by SCM Press Ltd
56 Bloomsbury Street London WC1

© SCM Press Ltd 1976

Type set by Gloucester Typesetting Co Ltd
and printed in Great Britain by
Fletcher & Son Ltd
Norwich

CONTENTS

PREFACE

> Literary rogues great and small have struck gold with the Commune and have exploited it to the full. There is not a hack who has not churned out his slapdash pamphlet, book or History . . .*

This, written in 1871 by the Frenchman Lissagaray, should stand framed on the desk of every would-be commentator. Although Lissagaray was referring to treatment of the communes of revolutionary France, today's communes are also the subject of great interest and curiosity. A steady stream of books, written from both the inside and the outside of modern communes, has issued from publishers on both sides of the Atlantic. Journals about communes and community living have also appeared.

Why *this* book? It results from research sponsored largely by the World Council of Churches through their Ecumenical Scholarship Scheme. The subject of the research was the spate of new Christian communities in Western Europe, called here 'Christian Communes'. To take Western Europe as a whole is not to skate over local differences, but it cannot be denied that its various countries have much in common in their economic systems, social priorities and in the status accorded to what is known as religion. By Christian communes I am referring largely to the communities which have sprung up since the late sixties, not entirely dissimilar to earlier communities but yet constituting an identifiable phenomenon.

A great many people have given me encouragement, believing as I do that something significant is happening. I am grateful to those who administer the World Council of Churches Scholarship Scheme and particularly to Winifred Chaplin, Scholarships Secretary of Christian Aid, who is responsible for World Council of Churches Scholarships in this country. Additional financial assistance was given by the World Council of Churches Writers' Project Fund on the recommendation of the Rev. Rex Davis of the World Council of

* Quoted by D. and G. Cohn-Bendit, *Obsolete Communism; The Left-Wing Alternative*, Penguin Books 1969, p. 8.

Churches Renewal Group, and by the Woods Paton Tatlow Memorial Funds on the recommendation of Canon David Paton.

I was singularly lucky in the willing superviser appointed by the Scholarship Scheme to guide the research project. This was the Rev. F. B. Welbourn, Senior Lecturer in Religious Studies at the University of Bristol. His piercing questions largely suggested the course taken by the research, but I do not of course want to imply his complete agreement with what actually resulted.

Much to my benefit I was taken under the wing of the British Council of Churches Youth Unit whose then secretary, the Rev. Roger Nunn, supplied an office and invaluable contacts both here and abroad. He also patiently read successive drafts of the research and suggested improvements, many of which were adopted. His colleagues Sally Barnes, Judy Coleman, Geoffery Corry and Sheila Prosper also gave considerable assistance.

At various times during the whole enterprise I learnt much from conversations with many friends, but especially with David Paton and Rex Davis, and with Bob and Maggi Whyte who were then on the staff of the Student Christian Movement. These all read the manuscript and made numerous very helpful comments. Any errors of fact or naiveté of judgment which remain are mine alone. It ought to be added that the research expresses my own opinions only and not the official stand of any of the organizations mentioned.

The communities who so generously opened their doors to me are more difficult to thank since their contribution is so fundamental. Suffice it to say that if I have misrepresented them in any way this was the result of enthusiasm rather than dishonesty.

I am most grateful to Catharine English who typed the manuscript and to Linda Foster who prepared it for publication.

As for my wife, she made it all possible, married me in spite of the project and was relentlessly critical at every stage.

December 1975   Andrew Lockley

1

Christian Communes

Christian communities are as old as Christianity.

> Now the company of those who believed were of one heart and soul, and
> no one said that any of the things which he possessed was his own, but
> they had everything in common. And with great power the apostles gave
> their testimony to the resurrection of the Lord Jesus, and great grace was
> upon them all. There was not a needy person among them, for as many
> as were possessors of lands or houses sold them, and brought the proceeds
> of what was sold and laid it at the apostles' feet; and distribution was
> made to each as any had need.[1]

We can't tell from this passage from the Acts of the Apostles
whether these early Christians actually lived in what we would call
communes. Nor does it matter. But later Christians have been
inspired by this model of the Christian life and some of them have
chosen to live in communes.

The communes of the past few years are of course by no means
the first residential Christian communities. From early on in the
history of the church the monastic orders' primary structure was the
communal group. But not only the monastic orders; others have
also been attracted to the community model as a way of living. After
the Reformation these included not only Catholics but some Protestants who, with Catholic monasticism closed to them, formed
another kind of Christian community which was able to include
families.

Two of the earliest of these communities in Britain illustrate the
breadth of community models. The Little Gidding community[2] was
founded in 1625 by the Anglican mystic, Nicholas Ferrar, who
retired from public life to bury himself in the country. The community grew to thirty people, placing a particular emphasis on the
rhythm of work and worship. (In 1972 another family started a new
community at Little Gidding; see below.)

By contrast the Diggers, who began during the Civil War shortly after the Little Gidding community, were fiercely committed to the political issues of the day. Their question was 'Why may we not have our Heaven here (that is a comfortable livelihood in the earth) and Heaven hereafter too?'[3] From their communities, first in Weybridge and then on Cobham Common, their leader Gerrard Winstanley wrote: 'seeing the common people of England, by joint consent of person and purse, have cast out Charles . . . the land now is to return into the joynt hands of those who have conquered, that is the commonours.'

The victory over King Charles was incomplete, he argued, as long as 'we remayne slaves still to the kingly power in the hands of lords of manors'.[4]

The Diggers' communities and Little Gidding were very different from one another. While Little Gidding was born out of an urge to withdraw into rural solitude the Diggers played an active part in the central political question of the day, that of who should govern England. Today, too, it is not difficult to find both 'religious' and 'secular' communities with practical commitments as wide apart as those of Little Gidding and the Diggers.

Little Gidding and the Diggers were both *Christian* communities. It would be surprising in the seventeenth century if they were not. And indeed, up to the nineteenth century 'secular' communities were unheard of. But with the growth of the influence of so-called utopian socialists like Robert Owen, blueprints for ideal communities were drawn up (and sometimes put into practice) which acknowledged no debt to Christianity. Now over a century later 'secular' communities are commonplace.

At the same time communities based consciously on the precepts of Christianity have continued to flourish. Tolstoy, the great Russian writer, found his ideas taken up by communal idealists, both Christian and non-Christian. The Doukhobors,[5] for example, though originating in the Ukraine in the eighteenth century, adopted the pacifist and anti-nationalist opinions of Tolstoy and moved to Canada. They called themselves the 'Christian Commune of the Universal Brotherhood' and disdained membership of any earthly state. Then there were the flourishing communities of Anabaptists, including the Hutterites (who are said still to have 164 communities in the United States of America), and the Amish Mennonites. The origins of the Hutterites lie far back in state persecutions in Reformation Switzerland. They have been joined by other communal groups at various times. One of their most recent associations was with the Bruderhof founded by Eberhard Arnold, one-time secretary of the German Student Christian Movement.[6]

While all this has been going on, the monastic orders of the Roman Catholic and Orthodox Churches have continued to thrive. Indeed, the attraction of that model of Christian community has been such that during the nineteenth and twentieth centuries it has spread to the Protestant Churches of Western Europe. In the Anglican Church, for example, a flurry of activity towards the end of the last century produced several women's orders and three very influential men's orders. Like long-established orders they wore habits. They kept a rhythm of work and worship and took vows of poverty, chastity and obedience. The men's orders, the Society of St John the Evangelist, the Community of the Resurrection and the Society of the Sacred Mission, all became involved in the new situations of human need brought about by the Industrial Revolution.[7] Monasticism has since also found its way into the Protestant denominations elsewhere in Europe. In Germany there are the Marienschwester and in Switzerland the Communauté de Grandchamp, which is closely linked with the Taizé community in France.

Taizé, probably the best-known of the modern monasteries, was founded by Roger Schutz (later its Prior) towards the end of the Second World War. In its taking of vows of poverty, chastity and obedience and in maintaining a daily rhythm of life the community is thoroughly traditional. Although originally an example of monasticism within a Protestant denomination it became the first ecumenical monastic community.[8]

But in fact the boundary between so-called 'monastic communities' and other Christian residential communities is becoming less clear. Some recently founded communities which do not call themselves monastic, nevertheless take lifelong vows and maintain a rhythmic daily pattern similar to monastic communities. The Laurentiuskonvent, described in chapter 3, is one such community.

During this century there has indeed been a steady stream of new Christian communities outside the monastic tradition, but not entirely dissimilar to it. Some have become well-established, and have lasted, others have thrived temporarily and then faded away. Among those established groups whose names are best known are the Iona and Focolare communities. Iona is not a year-round residential community. Its members live together during the summer on the island of Iona, off the west coast of Scotland, but the community is committed to a rule covering prayer, time and money which takes effect all the year round.

The Focolare, on the other hand, are full-time communitarians. Though Italian in origin, they have more than forty communities all over the world. The Focolare is a wide-open movement with a place for those who cannot commit themselves to living communally, but it is in their residential communities that their spirit finds its most concrete expression. (The word Focolare comes from the Italian for 'hearth', incidentally.) The aim of the *Focolarini* (as the Focolare members are known) is to live fully the love and unity taught by Christ and thus to renew the church and society.[9]

Thus the communitarian picture up until the later years of the 1960s was made up of monastic communities, old and new, some other Christian communities not giving themselves the 'monastic' title, and the occasional 'secular' community.

But at the end of the sixties there was a mushrooming of communal experiments. These were known by a variety of names, communes, communities, community houses. This was a largely 'secular' development in the first instance, but Christians were involved in some of these experiments and soon an increase in the number of Christian communities took place also.

This mushrooming of communities took place all over Western Europe and America. Figures estimating totals vary wildly, but they give some idea of the size of the phenomenon. One writer quotes some estimates: over 2,000 rural and several thousand urban communes in the United States of America in 1970, approximately 200 communities led by Roman Catholic religious in Holland in 1969, and (his own estimate) 100 communal ventures of various types in Britain in 1972.[10] An article in an American newspaper in 1970 mentioned that it too had found 2,000 rural communes in the United States of America, but another estimate for the same year put the figure at only 500.[11]

The wide variation in the figures for America highlights the difficulty of defining a 'commune' or 'community'. When is a group of people living together a community? For the purposes of this book the answer is 'when they are an intentional community'; in other words when they have made a conscious decision to create a community.

But why the growth of interest in communal living in the past few years? It has often been the case in the past that communal groups have represented a minority viewpoint in their time. Their life in community has performed a number of functions. Community life has been a way of strengthening that minority against the pressures of conformity to a wider society. Communities have also acted as retreats from the excessive pressures of day-to-day existence. Sometimes they have been models of a utopian society. Sometimes they have been revolutionary cells, or agents for social or political activism.

These various functions of community living fitted well the conditions of the late sixties and early seventies in which mainly youthful minorities developed biting critiques of Western society. Here a little history is called for.

The year 1967 saw the arrival of the 'hippy'. This word was originally invented (by a San Francisco newspaper columnist) to describe groups of young people who had established informal experiments in communal living in the Haight Ashbury district of San Francisco. Haight Ashbury was aptly renamed Hashbury, aptly because of its reputation as a centre for those who smoked the drug cannabis. Another play on the name was the slogan 'Haight means love'. A similar slogan of that place and time, 'Make love not war' found an echo all over the world. The spirit of the hippies was quickly appreciated by other young people, and by big business. 'Hippy' clothes and records poured forth and already in 1967 Scott Mackenzie's record 'San Francisco (where the flowers grow very high)' had reached the top of the charts throughout the world.

However, 1968 brought very different events. Violent riots emanating from French universities were followed by upheaval among students all over the world, and led indirectly to the downfall of the government of General de Gaulle in France. The protest was precipitated by the state of education in certain European countries but led to involvement in issues far wider than this, including protest against the Americans' activities in Indo-China. Some indeed were opposed to the most basic assumptions of Western capitalist society.[12]

In these two successive years events in San Francisco and Paris crystallized attitudes, very different attitudes, which some young people shared over against the wider society. These attitudes were, however, very much minority viewpoints and communes appeared, performing the various functions they had earlier performed for other minority viewpoints.[13] The communal picture has been constantly changing as the issues have shifted or gained different emphases and the people involved have developed. Newcomers have arrived;

others have dropped out. Communes have come and gone. There is no coherence about it.[14]

The general growth in communes has brought with it an increase in the number of Christian communities, and since the late sixties there have been many experiments which could be described as Christian communes. Some have died after a shorter or longer life; others have existed for some years. This book describes five communities in detail, four of which have been founded since the late sixties.

What are Christian communes and where are they to be found?

A significant minority is buried deep in the country. Some of these attempt to farm, like a commune in the depopulated north of Norway which farms for its subsistence. The intentions of those involved in the Greenbus community in England (see chapter 4) are to make farming their main occupation. In other rural communities growing things is only part of their intention. The Lord's Family in Bavaria grows vegetables and lives on them but it also makes music and films. And the Kingsway community, originally solely an urban community in London whose work is among those whom society casts off, acquired the use of a farm in Cornwall in 1973 and now hopes to maintain both its urban and its rural links.[15]

The 1970s' version of the Little Gidding community in East Anglia would be expressing the hopes of many rural groups when it writes:

> We live on an eight-acre plot in an area which has suffered from rural depopulation. We are surrounded by mammoth farms owned by property trusts, insurance companies and ecclesiastical bodies. The farming is heavily mechanized, almost entirely arable, and relies largely on the use of chemicals.
>
> Out of our tiny acreage we plan to grow naturally enough vegetables to feed ourselves and our many visitors. We have started with hens for eggs and meat, and we hope to move on to keeping a cow or goats for milk, butter and cheese, fish in our two ponds and possibly a horse or donkey to help us with the work. We want to learn about using the sun and wind and sewage for power and heat. We shall plant trees for fuel, nuts, fruit and sheer beauty.[16]

Behind all these different ventures is an urge to shun the city and return to a way of life which is simple, healthy and in tune and in touch with nature. Ecological considerations are of prime importance. Certain other communities live in the country, but do not

make their living from farming. The Emmaus Community in Langeweg, Holland (see chapter 2), is rurally isolated, and though its
emphasis too is on simplicity of life-style, it expresses this not in
farming of any kind, but in a rag-and-bone business. It collects and
sells perfectly usable goods which others have thrown out. Like the
Kingsway community, the Greenbus community and many others,
Emmaus tries to maintain an open door to anyone needing food,
shelter or care.

A different kind of community but still rural is the Wick community near Bristol. At the time of writing this community's future
is uncertain, but it has been made up of the headquarters staff of the
Student Christian Movement, who decided that to work properly as
a team it was necessary to live as a communal unit. Of its nature this
community is essentially an outgoing one, concerned with work
among students.

Communities, equally outgoing, but with an entirely different
approach to the needs of the individual are those whose main concern is evangelism. Within the past few years some young people
have committed themselves to communities established with evangelism as their prime concern. The Children of God started a chain
of communes across Western Europe including a number in the
British Isles. The Jesus Liberation Front set themselves up in Hemel
Hempstead, the Jesus Family in south London.[17] Other communities
with a more local orientation but similar activities include Christian
Fellowship House in Birmingham and the Addison House Community in Hull. The latter has considerable involvement also in local
youth- and play-groups.

Representative of an approach to the individual which is different
again is OZ100 in the 'red-light district' of Amsterdam, Holland.
This community attempts the pastoral care of the varied individuals
who live around them, but at the same time attempts to work at the
problems of the area as a whole. Two of the chief of these are home-
lessness and the lack of provision for the large local communities of
Moroccans and others with Arab origins who have come to Amsterdam for work. OZ100 has enabled the establishing of educational
facilities in order that these Arabs may learn in their native tongue
and about their own culture.

An ordained minister and a priest are prominent in the ecumenical
OZ100. Clergymen of different denominations have also been prominent in other communities founded over the last ten years, including
the Bread and Fishes Community of Sweden (whose work is not

dissimilar to that of Emmaus, Langeweg) and the Aarhus Open Family of Denmark. This latter community is part of a wider group which has formed around the Aarhus Ecumenical Centre. The Open Family is a group of about eighty adults and children who have decided to share their lives without yet being a residential community. They work in common for and with the university in Aarhus, camp together during the summer and have certain common financial arrangements. One community which has won much acclaim for its ecumenical work is the Corrymeela Community of Northern Ireland, deeply involved in the work of reconciliation between Protestant and Catholic.[18]

The process of 'collectivization' on which the Open Family has embarked is similar to that of the OPUS group in Glasgow, who share their weekends in a farmhouse they have renovated for wider use, and the Ashram Community of England. Though the Ashram Community is primarily a group of individuals and families who have committed themselves to a common quest for an authentic Christian life-style, to pledged giving and a devotional discipline, the Community has also sponsored community houses. The first Ashram Houses have been in inner-city areas in Sheffield, Rochdale and Teesside where their residents work as social or community workers, teachers, ministers and so on.[19] Very similar in ethos to the Ashram Houses but having no organizational link are the Shenley House Community and Sparkbrook Community House, both in Birmingham.

Communities whose aim is urban involvement are not new. The Roman Catholic tradition produced La Poudrière in Brussels and L'Isolotto in Florence in the 1950s. Something is said about L'Isolotto and other so-called *communita di base* in Italy in chapter 5. In Britain two communities with a similar emphasis grew out of the Student Christian Movement at the end of the 1960s, Newhaven in Edinburgh and Blackheath in London.[20] Blackheath folded after two years and Newhaven has changed since its early days, but both started from the members' commitment to local political issues and the needs of the areas in which they lived. These communes aimed to promote radical social change. Cinisello, an Italian group described in chapter 5, shares these ambitions.

Finally there are the loosely-knit groups of young people sharing a house, housework and expenses, sometimes with common activities and a eucharist. The British and Irish Student Christian Movement put up the money for a number of communities like this in 1973 and

1974 and one of them is described in chapter 6. Similar experiments exist all over Western Europe (many have grown out of the influence of Taizé also) particularly in university towns. There is only a thin line between this sort of group and groups of friends who happen to live in the same building and who share some of their resources without having made a decision to live communally. Whether the latter can accurately be described as 'communities depends on one's definitions. Using the word to mean 'intentional' community as defined above they would fall outside the definition.

There are of course many other Christian communes in Western Europe; those mentioned above are only a representative sample of the wide variety of experiments at present in existence. In the same way the five communities described in greater detail in the following five chapters are only a representative sample. They were deliberately chosen as five very different experiments. Two are rural, two urban and one suburban. Their main activities vary from rag-and-bone collection to teaching. Some include families, others only the unmarried. Their confessional traditions vary also, as does their ecumenicity. One community is entirely made up of members from one denomination; another is so ecumenical that its members are virtually non-denominational. Special factors applied to two of the communities. One longer-established community provides a comparison with more recently-founded groups (and the contrast is explored in chapter 9). Another of the five experiments was only starting when I visited it and that factor enabled me to go into its early history as it was happening.

The five descriptive chapters follow on one another without comment, which is reserved for the later chapters.

2

The Emmaus Community
Langeweg, Netherlands

Langeweg is a tiny and unremarkable Dutch village. Even the name
means only 'Long Road'. The village almost matches the English
stereotype of the Netherlands, for it has dykes, tulips in spring, and
lies in rich land of unrelenting flatness. Only a windmill is missing.

This tranquillity, however, is not to be found in the Dutch nation
as a whole. A society which until the Second World War was almost
unrivalled in Europe for its stability, was badly shaken by the German occupation. The pillars of that stability had been 'denominational' blocs – Calvinist, Roman Catholic and the secular Socialist
bloc – which had not only determined the individual's religion, but
also the party he voted for, the union he belonged to, the school he
went to and the newspaper he read. These separate pillars (*Zuilen*) in
Dutch society did not conflict, but managed to share political
power.

Since the war, the denominational blocs have continued, but with
decreased importance. Another symbol of Dutch stability – the
empire – has gone altogether; there remains only a slightly sour
taste and a large influx of coloured immigrants. Holland stands as
one of the countries of the European Economic Community, one of
the richest capitalist nations on earth, and one of the most densely
populated. The Dutch are not quite sure which direction they are
going in. They have lost both the clear identity of the *Zuilen* and
their sense of national purpose as an imperial power. In this uncertainty Holland has thrown up a number of significant social
developments so that the Dutch now have a reputation for liberal
innovations in fields as diverse as penal reform, aid to the Third
World and mental health.

In British press reports of Dutch affairs over the past decade,
perhaps two developments in particular have excited comment. The

first of these was the rise and fall of the two youth movements, the Provos and Kabouters. The appearance of the Provos in 1965 marked the first time that a part of European youth – already so much cultivated by the marketing men – finally asserted itself with both stringent criticisms of its parents' society and imaginative suggestions about change. One of the Provos' more successful enterprises was their 'white bicycle plan'. A large number of free bicycles were put at the disposal of Amsterdam's citizens. They had no locks and the intention was that they should be used for as long as an individual needed and then left for the next user. The Provos hoped to contribute to the solution of the inner-city transport problem and attacked the 'anti-social idol of the enslaved consumer, his car'.[1]

The second development to have excited particular comment has been the emergence of married Roman Catholic priests. The churches in the Netherlands have been under considerable challenge from both inside and outside their membership. In the Roman Catholic Church priests who have married and yet continued to exercise their priestly functions have become a symbol of the challenge to former certainties. But married priests are only the most spectacular characteristic of Holland's changing churches.[2] Another significant development has been the emergence in considerable numbers of informal religious communities. Holland has always had Roman Catholic monastic orders, but Protestant communities were unheard of. Of the many new communities some are formed by members of Catholic orders leaving their monasteries and convents and starting their own smaller communities. Many groups have formed also of those from largely Protestant backgrounds, some fifty of which maintain close connections with the Dutch Reformed Church. This is a development which has taken place largely since the mid-sixties.

One of these new communities – it includes two members of Catholic orders – is the Emmaus community in that unremarkable Dutch village, Langeweg. The largest building in Langeweg is a former Roman Catholic seminary adjacent to the village church and now given over to the Emmaus community.

The seminary used a large house, outhouses, a building which looks educational, the five acres of land attached and the church. Emmaus uses neither the educational building nor the church. From the outside the impression would have been much the same in 1970 – before Emmaus arrived – except that now at the gate is the new name and the symbol of the community, two hands reaching out for a piece of broken bread. The house itself is spartan—draughty and with high ceilings and long corridors. The outhouses are crammed with junk – furniture, clothes, bric-a-brac, electrical goods and books. There is a room piled to the ceiling with bales of clothing and another, specially built by the community, for sorting the tons of clothing which pass through Emmaus each week. Some hens and a herb garden remind the visitor that this is a rural community.

Emmaus is in the rag-and-bone business. The community collects and sorts everything that the neighbouring towns and villages throw out. It sells the best junk in its own market every Saturday; the less good junk is bought in bales by the Dutch recycling industry. Nearly everything in the house and on the members of the community is second-hand – clothes, furniture, kitchen utensils, carpets, bedding, TV, stereogram, fridge. In 1973 the community netted about £17,000 from this business.

This £17,000 is not achieved merely for the benefit of the community members. Every penny possible is sent to some four Third World projects which Emmaus supports leaving only the barest minimum to keep the community, the house, and their ancient van and car. The division of the takings, between the projects and the community, is roughly fifty-fifty. These four projects are in Papua-New Guinea, Brazil, South Africa and Indonesia. Personal links have been established with people working on all four projects. In addition, good clothes carefully selected for the appropriate climates are weeded out and sent at Emmaus' expense to the community's project contacts instead of being baled for recycling or sold at Emmaus' own market.

Emmaus, Langeweg, is one of about forty Emmaus communities throughout the world. The first Emmaus community was founded by a French priest, Abbé Pierre, in Paris in 1947. Its first aim was to provide a place where the homeless could find shelter but financial stringency soon forced the community to look for work. 'Ragpicking' was originally chosen because it was something everybody was capable of doing.[3]

The number living in Emmaus, Langeweg, is not constant. While I was there there were thirteen but others stayed for a few days, or a weekend, or came only to help at the Saturday market. None of these was local and all were young. The thirteen were of ages ranging from nineteen to the fifties, all single, men and women. Two had been at Emmaus since it began in Easter 1971. One of these was a Capuchin Franciscan in his fifties, the other was about thirty and the leader of the group. A third – a Franciscan nun of fifty – joined them soon after the community began. Both Franciscans have permission from their superiors to be at Emmaus.

The other ten did not expect to be so permanent. Most of these were young adults who had deliberately sought out Emmaus' life-style. Some had heard about it from the brothers of the Taizé community; others on the Dutch grapevine. These ten had no common pattern to their lives; some intended to receive further education of some sort. Two had given up jobs, one as a bricklayer and one as a teacher, and were looking for an alternative to these. Emmaus was the only one of the five communities described in this book with a largely international membership, including a Scot, a Dane, a German and a Belgian. The Belgian was one of four older members of the community (all male), who, after some domestic troubles or serious illness, were homeless. All Emmaus residents have equal membership of the community while they are there. There is no feeling that those who have been in the community longest are 'more' members than the others. This equality of membership is bolstered by one of the three rules of the community:

> Any allusion to the past of any member of the community is considered a serious mistake and must be repaired without delay. Everybody is accepted as the human being he is, regardless of his origin, his past or his ideas.

Everyone has come to Emmaus for a different reason, everyone has come because he needs something. Nobody asks the reason, everyone accepts the person. There is no charity here, no servers or served, no helpers and helped. Nobody is forced into the role of giver or receiver.

If false roles are not forced on members of the group they are free to be of mutual support to each other, through common work, common meals, common worship and just being together. But there is also the experience of the person who wrote on a graffiti-sheet which hangs in the entrance hall: 'It is possible to feel terribly alone with ten people'.

Common life is central to community life. But the extent to which life is common differs from community to community. At Emmaus everybody lives in the same building. Most of life is shared.

The central feature of this shared life is the rag-and-bone trade. This is what earns the community its daily bread, even for those who do not spend every day working at it. For as well as the collection, sorting and baling of second-hand goods, the house and property must be maintained, the shopping and washing must be done and letters must be written. Whatever the members of the community are actually working on they do at least six hours a day between regular hours.

The community aims to be as self-sufficient as possible though it cannot grow much of its own food. The full use of all the skills of the members entails that help from the outside is minimal. Self-sufficiency is also enshrined in the second of the community's rules: 'Nobody shall depend on anything other than his work for his subsistence'. The community has no capital and any gifts it receives are charitably used.

Emmaus' philosophy of work is strikingly different from that of ordinary capitalist enterprises. No employer lives off the sweat of the community's brow. It works for itself and for the world's needy, controlling, in Marx's phrase, the means of production and of distribution. Nobody joining the community must first prove his productivity potential. Everybody, the leader included, earns the same amount, board and lodging and £2.50 a week (fifteen guilders). Nobody earns, or is entitled to, more than that. Wages are not paid in proportion to productivity, efficiency, responsibility, but simply to a man or woman as a human being, equal in worth to all those he or she works with. Emmaus is a highly successful industry run on co-operative lines.

Because the hours of work are regular it is easy for everybody to take their meals together. This they do not only for breakfast, lunch and supper but also for mid-morning and afternoon breaks. Meals are simple but wholesome, with plenty of brown bread and vegetables. There is a rota for work in the kitchen both in the week and at weekends, and this is divided equally between men and women. In order that the person who works in the kitchen shall work the same regular hours as those for example sorting clothes, the washing-up is postponed until after the after-lunch siesta. The regular, rhythmic pattern of activity is held to be important and though the work is often repetitive it appears to be also satisfying since it is performed with a rare joy and verve.

The twice daily opportunity for meditative worship is part of this rhythmic pattern. Indeed, it is seen as so important that in theory those who are not prepared to join the community's meditative life may only stay until their basic needs for food and shelter are met. (In practice nobody is actually asked to leave.) Before breakfast and supper many of the community gather in a dark well-carpeted room whose walls are covered with drapes. The room is quiet; candles blaze. There are only cushions and very low stools to sit on. Many take off their shoes and sit cross-legged in the yoga lotus position. Everybody tries to stay as quiet as possible.

The act of worship might begin with recorded music, conducive to silent meditation. A theme might then be introduced by the person leading the worship – usually the friar – and be developed in Bible readings, thoughts, prayers and songs. These themes often spring from the experience of the group as a community sharing work, ideals, pleasures and pain. But there is not always a theme, nor any regular structure. Once we listened to Bach for three-quarters of an hour with a reading of Mark 12.41–44 in the middle. This is the story of the widow who contributed all that she had, although it was very little, to the temple offerings. Often during these acts of worship the eucharist will be celebrated, particularly on special days like the birthday or departure of a community member. Different rites will be used but always the friar, who is ordained, will celebrate and the bread and wine will be passed from one to another.

The pace of the meditative worship is slow and relaxing. The content is thought-provoking and two ideas are dominant; the relationship between God and the individual and the role of the community itself as a 'light' to the rest of society. The community sees itself as a model within the larger society but it does not assert this either conceitedly or self-consciously.

There is little contact between the community and the parish church next door. The Catholic parish priest appears occasionally with junk he has collected for the community but the community does not attend services at the church. At Emmaus one has to look very hard to find any of the usual consciousness of denomination, even among Dutch members, and even among those who are Catholics. One might expect at least the Catholics within the community to have some link with the parish church. But at Emmaus it is more important to the members that they are members of the community than that they are members of a denomination. As a corollary to this members of Emmaus take communion together as a community and not as members of their parish church.

Lunch and supper are also accompanied by devotions. A grace is improvised before lunch and the leader of the community (see below) always reads aloud two short texts, one biblical, the other from a modern religious thinker, before lunch ends. And at the end of supper the group usually sings a modern Dutch rendering of the Lord's Prayer.

A birthday was an opportunity for the community to celebrate. On their birthday each community member was the centre of attention. Fidelis, the nun, had a birthday while I was there and everybody, instead of buying presents, contributed something to the celebrations. Fidelis received very few presents indeed but other gifts made her happy; the embraces of others in the community, dolls made up to look like nuns, greenery on the table, a song specially written and the sudden urge to dance after supper round and round the table.

Everybody has his or her own room, though those with large ones must expect to share them if the house gets too full. Rooms are simple and furnished only with second-hand goods; carpets, bedding, pictures. When one is constantly sharing one's life with others in the group the chance to retire in privacy is greatly valued. There is also a common living room, with an atmosphere of warmth and ease, amply fitted out with others' throw-outs; a piano, a stereogram, easy chairs, soft mattresses, small tables.

Each person has his own possessions in his own room but these are usually very simple. Occasionally someone in the group will pick out a piece of clothing for himself or the whole group will find a piece of furniture, a picture or something similar which they will be able to use on the property. If, on rare occasions, anything new is acquired it will be paid for out of the earnings of the community. Most goods, being second-hand, are the property of all the members anyway. The way in which a community shares its goods depends often on the way the community is organized. Emmaus lives off the work it does together and not wages which individuals bring in. The wealth which the community creates for itself is used for running the business and paying the wages. This is a form of community of goods, since all put an equal effort into the work and draw equal benefits out.

Each of the Emmaus communities[4] is entirely independent and self-sufficient both as regards finance and decision-making, but up to now each has had a leader entitled *le responsable* (the one who is responsible). Much of the day-to-day organization like job allocation and the financial arrangements of the community are in the hands of this man. Emmaus does not shrink from having a treasurer or indeed a bank account. Nor is the community frightened of organization. The process by which the clothes are sorted and baled has been thought out according to the criteria of efficiency and profitability; without this, the Third World projects which depend on Emmaus, Langeweg, would suffer. No material is thrown away; even shreds of rags, which are much less profitable to the community than good wool or cotton, are baled for recycling.

Although many practical decisions are made as they come up by those who need to make them, and the hand of guidance is not much in evidence, those three members of the community who have been there longest carry with them an authority which comes from experience. Nobody seems to worry about 'Who runs this?' or 'Who runs that?'. Somehow this style of community obviates crises of leadership. This is probably because the community is conscious of a clear purpose and direction. Its members are as unanimous about these as thirteen diverse individuals could ever be. Emmaus' purpose and direction have their practical expression in the daily rhythm, which everybody accepts.

Someone has written on the graffiti-sheet in the hallway 'Living against the tide of the rest of humanity'. The phrases 'Living against the tide' and 'Being a sign of contradiction', both of which were frequently heard during the preparation for the Council of Youth which opened at Taizé in 1974,[5] vividly express Emmaus' view of itself. The whole style and purpose of the community's life is a non-violent protest against certain Western values and a pointing to the way life could be. Their symbolic protest against a consumption and consumerism which makes the very words 'rag-and-bone' outdated is to collect cast-offs and send the proceeds to those whom the rich world robs of its basic commodities. In its own words:

> We believe that picking up the vomit of our welfare state has the following significance: the left-overs of our prosperity are made use of for others who have nothing. That is the least we can do, and no more than an act of common decency. It asks us to go further. It continuously holds before our eyes the awful stupidity of the difference between our richness and the poverty of so many others. It inspires a whole simplicity and sobriety in the midst of a society which drives us more and more to want things, and never to be satisfied. Therefore we collect left-overs.[6]

Add to this the style of Emmaus' common living and worship and it is no wonder that they feel like a lone wave against the flow of the tide.

This isolation in thought is also an isolation in fact. Emmaus has as little contact with the world around it as many religious orders.

Such contacts as there are are mainly the business transactions involved in the junk trade. The most important of these is the Saturday market. A crowd of local people starts to form outside the gates of the community before 2 p.m. when the market begins. They position themselves as advantageously as possible, then, when the gates are opened, promptly at 2 p.m., in they run, fighting to reach the best bargains first. The picture is a vivid one; Emmaus removes its breakwater to the tide of the rest of humanity.

As the tide flows round the outhouses of the property (if one may retain the metaphor), no opportunity is missed to convey the purpose of the Emmaus community to them as they spend on average £250 per week. On the wall of the room selling second-hand books is written 'Help us in our work for those who are poorest'. This is also expressed in the third rule of the community: 'The purpose of our work is to help others in need, in order to serve real peace'. The peace theme is prominent. The observant shopper notices the peace symbol adopted by the Campaign for Nuclear Disarmament moulded in concrete on the ground. It also appears round the house. He also sees a poster portraying a black man almost on his knees looking upwards saying simply 'Peace, brother'. In the kitchen, which most shoppers are unlikely to penetrate, there are two complementary symbols – a crucifix and a poster. The poster bears the head and shoulders of a long-haired and scruffy looking young man and the inscription: 'Wanted – Jesus Christ, Son of God, King of Kings-Prince of Peace'. Among the crimes for which he is wanted are prac‚ tising medicine and distributing food without the necessary licences, and interfering with business men in the temple. The notice ends: 'This man is dangerous, especially to young people who have not yet learned to ignore him. Warning: He is still at large'. This is the Dutch version of a poster seen in many countries and many languages.

Emmaus Langeweg's style is one appropriate to all the countries of the Western world. Although it would be equally appropriate in Britain Emmaus has grown strong in the present climate in the Netherlands. This community is an example of a practical alternative which is both satisfying to its members and of service to others.

3

The Laurentiuskonvent
West Germany

The most notable fact about modern West Germany is the speed with which it has risen again from the wholesale devastation of the Second World War. So much so that by the standards of modern capitalism the Federal Republic is either at the top or near the top of the league tables of gross national product, average income of citizens, strength of currency and number of motorways per square kilometre.

Such facts are impressive to some. And they are facts in which many Germans take a great pride. Economic success is seen as making amends for the evils of the thirties and forties. To the visitor it also seems that economic success has another significance. Material and industrial rivalry is the competition between the West Germans and their other half in the East, the German Democratic Republic, in which the prize of victory is the justification of the system of the winner.

A whole new generation has grown up in Germany which did not live through the Second World War. It feels neither compulsion to make amends for National Socialism nor any desperate loyalty to the social democracy of the Federal Republic. Tension between the generations seems to me more noticeable here than in other European nations. The young do nothing to discourage their elders' feeling of responsibility for the horrors of Nazism; the old suspect that the young are eager to upset the social democracy, which was born from their collective guilt.

Guilt rankled particularly in the Protestant Church of Germany, part of which (the so-called German Christians) had sided with Hitler. Six months after the end of the war German Protestants declared in the Stuttgart Confession of Guilt: 'We reproach ourselves that we did not bear witness more courageously, did not pray more

faithfully, did not believe more joyfully and did not love more
ardently . . . Now a new beginning must be made in our churches.
. . .'[1] The church had come apart at the seams during the 1930s
dividing down lines of support or opposition to Hitler's policies to
the church. The so-called Confessing Church (*Bekennente Kirche*)
opposed Nazi interference in church affairs and its leaders were
rewarded with imprisonment and in some cases, death.

Although the Confessing Church no longer exists its spirit still
permeates German Protestantism. Many are still conscious of its
witness under ghastly privations, treating that as a standard against
which to measure their own church. For contemporary Germans it
is not so much the fight against state interference which is of immediate relevance. It is rather the belief that the church should take a
political stand and should rediscover the meaning of community.
Opposition to Hitler had marked a watershed for the traditionally
a-political Protestant Churches in Germany. German Protestants,
previously taking their justification from Luther's doctrine of the
two kingdoms, had maintained a complete divorce between the
church and politics. The gospel did not relate to man's public
behaviour. The Confessing Church however was forced by the
presence of Nazism to bring the gospel into the political arena. And
in the Confessing Church's seminary at Finkenwalde Dietrich Bonhoeffer had worked out a model residential Christian community, a
rare venture in the German Protestant Church.[2]

Among those who have maintained the renewing spirit of the
Confessing Church in the greatly altered post-war situation is the
Laurentiuskonvent community. Indeed one of their number was
once linked with Finkenwalde. A statement by the Laurentiuskonvent shows its debt to the thinking of the Confessing Church. 'The
Laurentiuskonvent brings together Christians who are prepared by
means of binding forms to try to live a common life and service in
the spirit of Christ's gospel and thus to contribute to the renewal of
the church and the changing of the world.'[3]

At the foot of the hills on the right bank of the Rhine, almost opposite the Federal German capital, Bonn, lies the suburb of Römlinghoven. In Römlinghoven is a large and ancient complex of red-painted
buildings named the Malteserhof. This property is at present rented
by the Laurentiuskonvent.

The community began in 1959 when three single men decided to
live communally, sharing all that they had. Their student experiences

had awakened them to the possibility of this, and their resolve had been confirmed by the example of the Taizé community, where one of them had been a novice for two years. Since those early days, both single women and families have joined the community, making it the first experiment of its kind within the German church. When I lived with them there were thirteen members of Laurentiuskonvent at the Malteserhof and its annexe in North Bonn. All were over thirty. Of these, six were single men, who have made life vows of celibacy (brothers), three single women who have done the same (sisters) and four were married. These two couples have between them eight children who are not members of the Laurentiuskonvent.

These children cannot be members because membership of the Laurentiuskonvent is for life and nobody takes it for granted that the children of present members will want that. There are about another twenty members of the community who do not live at the Malteserhof, but it is the common life of the Malteserhof itself which is most significant.

The Laurentiuskonvent, though it has a common aim, avoids a single common task. The work on which members of the community are engaged is not constant and depends partly on the channels into which the community puts its energies. While previously it concentrated on the rehabilitation of boys convicted of criminal offences, it is at present orientated towards helping young volunteers who wish to contribute to peace-work. And indeed to work for peace is the main aim of the community. There are three different peace-work organizations run from the Malteserhof and staffed partly by members of the Laurentiuskonvent.

The community decides what job each of its members will do. Some work with the peace-work projects, while the others are at the present employed in the jobs of postman, carpenter, geologist, masseur and social workers. All must be prepared to practise professions different from those for which they trained; all must work at jobs compatible with peace-work. This means in practice, one of the brothers said, that members cannot be employed by the forces or manage 'ultra-capitalist enterprises'. So great a variety of occupations brings about a widely-spread influence. The community would rather have this than confine its energies to one particular shared task. This flexibility allows the Laurentiuskonvent to be ready for different kinds of work. The touchstone of their work is always: 'Does it promote peace?'.

What the community means by 'peace' needs some clarification. The community is continually adapting itself in order to reflect its growing understanding of this word. Peace means the opposite to war in the first instance. But to work for peace implies a stand not only against war but also against the use of violence. 'To be rigid about the use of violence may be a useful testimony for Christians in today's society, even if it is not rational to be so rigid,' says one of the Laurentiuskonvent's brothers. Thus the Christian will give an example by promoting and working for non-violent solutions to problems and conflicts. And if you believe, as the Laurentiuskonvent does, that real peace can only exist when men live together within just social structures then working for peace has implications for change in unjust social structures. Violence, they say, is built into our social structures. The Laurentiuskonvent see their vocation as Christians to work towards the realization of the peace which Christ left with the world in John 14.27. ('Peace I leave with you; my peace I give to you; not as the world gives do I give it to you.') The word 'peace', however understood, has a peculiar pointedness in a Germany humiliated in two wars.

The nature of the community's peace-work is most clear from the work of the three organizations whose base is currently at the Malteserhof. First, there is *Eirene, International Christian Service for Peace*, whose main function is to maintain two volunteer projects in Morocco and Zaire. Only pacifists (defined as 'those who stand for non-violent solutions to conflicts') and Christian pacifists at that, are accepted as volunteers. Secondly, there is *Aktionsgemeinschaft; Dienst für den Frieden* (Action Committee; Service for Peace), a co-ordinating organization for the ten Christian peace-groups working in Germany. This is financed almost entirely by the German Protestant Church and interprets its co-ordinating function widely. It acts as a clearing-house for the activities and projects of the ten groups. It represents their point of view to the government across the Rhine, particularly so far as the rights of conscientious objectors to military service are concerned. It publicizes their work in the media, keeps a well-stocked library and runs seminars on volunteers and peace-work. The third organization – *Kinder in Not* (Children in Need) – is a community project in North Bonn. Its work is mainly with children whose families have been rehoused, but who are disorientated and frustrated in their new surroundings. Community projects in Germany are not coping with real material deprivation, of which there is little. Deprivation takes other forms. Two young adults, travelling in Germany, preparing for the Council of Youth (which began at Taizé in 1974), wrote: 'Germany; materially such a rich country, with a high living standard, but the pain and suffering is there in a different way: a lot of isolation and loneliness, and often a desperate confusion under the surface of a well-organized existence.' *Kinder in Not* has also begun a project among homeless people in Cologne.

Young adults working with these organizations also live at the Malteserhof. Many of them are conscientious objectors who have refused to do National Service. Instead they must do sixteen months' social work; this is possible at the Malteserhof. Others are there because they wish to do voluntary service. Sometimes the Malteserhof also runs courses for volunteers about to go overseas, and these will be very temporarily resident at the Hof.

As a result of a significant event in 1973 the Laurentiuskonvent was able to clear its own mind on the question of what the vocation of working for peace means. At irregular intervals the German Protestant Church sponsors a *Kirchentag* – a bonanza of lay education unparalleled among European churches. At that held in Düsseldorf in 1973 the Laurentiuskonvent was delegated to organize a *Shalom*[4] Forum (a Peace-Forum) which brought together as in a market-place twenty-nine groups and many individuals involved in work for peace. Good press coverage enabled the *Shalom* Forum to reach a wide audience but the Laurentiuskonvent says that their work for it also showed them how their common life was already lived 'under the vocation of *Shalom*'. They see this common life as a three-part commitment – to each other as a group, to the world in service and to the reality of God in worship and celebration.

The Laurentiuskonvent's first commitment – to each other – is lifelong. This is only undertaken after a sort of novitiate in which both the applicant and the community size each other up.

The community calls itself a 'close-knit community of binding everyday-togetherness' and it lays great emphasis on sharing as much as possible. The members of the Laurentiuskonvent lay open to each other not only their spiritual life and worship but also their material life and political concerns. All these contribute to the day-to-day life of the community; by offering them to each other in love they bring them to Christ whom they believe should not be excluded from any sector of life.

This everyday-togetherness is well organized. Whatever job the members of Laurentiuskonvent do, they pool their salaries and their property. Each member then receives back DM100 a month (about £16.50). If an individual or family needs extra money for special expenses such as clothing or travel this is discussed by the whole community. Much of the rest of the money finances common house-keeping. But the Laurentiuskonvent sees it as an important part of its work to use its money to help individuals or finance tasks whose importance is not recognized by others.

All important decisions are made by the whole of the community together at its meeting on Friday nights and Saturday mornings. These decisions include those relating to finance and work, member-ship of the community, the particular problems of the Malteserhof, and such sundries as whether or not to allow a researcher to share their life. There is no voting and discussion continues until all members have agreed on a course acceptable to all. Although one of the brothers is called *Ältester der Kommunität* (Elder of the Com-munity) he has no power to take decisions on the community's behalf. If he is present he leads acts of worship (in chapel or at meals) but he has no special seat on any occasion.

Everybody on the Malteserhof, Laurentiuskonvent or others, eats together. This emphasizes that there exists also a community wider than that of the Laurentiuskonvent which shares its purpose. Only when the Laurentiuskonvent is having its weekly meeting does it closet itself away and eat and worship as a group. Meals are usually prepared by two elderly ladies who are also part of the wider group which lives on the Hof but everybody, regardless of sex, works in the kitchen at various times. The families sometimes eat separately but they eat the same food prepared in the same kitchen.

The families perhaps lead more of a separate existence than do the single members. A contributory factor is that only they have flats, while all the single people have bedsitters. The families are thus more self-contained. They also each have four children who look to their natural parents first, although they are exceptionally friendly to and open with the other adults. The community feels a common responsi-bility for the children, which makes it easier, for example, for a mother to go away for a few days. The children are still young. Later on will come the decision whether or not to become members of the community. One of the mothers mentioned to me the possibility of moving out for a few years in order to give the children more experience to help them decide. In such a case, the parents would remain full members of the Laurentiuskonvent although they would be living elsewhere.

The second part of the 'vocation of *Shalom*' is the Laurentiuskonvent's commitment to the world in service. Not every community
lays as much emphasis on being outward-looking; 'staying in solidarity' with the world, as the community puts it. Indeed the name
Laurentiuskonvent reflects what the community sees as its leaning
towards service. St Laurence was the founder of the Capuchin
Franciscans in Germany and, like all friars, is identified with self-
giving and working for others.

One of the Laurentiuskonvent's two aims is the changing of society.
'We know that to change society will not bring the kingdom of God
on earth. But we can't avoid responsibility for society. And because
things are changing very quickly and revolution is the nature of
today's existence, to take responsibility means to be revolutionary.'
In practice this seems to mean two things; that the Laurentiuskonvent is not a supporter of the *status quo* and that it gives much
attention to picking up the casualties of a fast-changing society. As
far as possible these are held in tension in the sponsoring of community work among the disorientated and the supply of volunteers
to African nations. The Laurentiuskonvent is also open as a community to all who need it: to a middle-aged gentleman convalescing
after severe psychiatric disturbance and brought to the Malteserhof
by the masseur; to a widow who arrived demanding shelter one
night and has stayed ever since; to those who lived with them when
their work was among the convicted young.

The Laurentiuskonvent has an outhouse area perfect for young
children. This is now equipped with broken-down cars, things to
climb on, paints and other creative materials, and one of the community's mothers organizes a play-group for the local children.
Although all except one of the Malteserhof children are now too old,
this continues.

'Our work and service could lead us to an existence without hope
if we did not set everything we are doing against a horizon of hope
and eschatology. The reality of God is wider than the reality we are
living out here.' In order to set themselves firmly within this wider
reality the third part of the Laurentiuskonvent's 'vocation of *Shalom*'
is a discipline of worship. Anyone at the Malteserhof may share this
if they wish. Three times a day the community gathers in the small,
simple chapel, decorated only by a cross, a candle and an icon. Two
of these services, at 7 a.m. and 6.30 p.m., are according to the Office
of the Laurentiuskonvent, for, like monastic orders, this community
also has an order of service for particular times of day. At the

Malteserhof these are different each day of the week. In addition at
10 a.m. there is a very short service mainly for those who cannot
manage the earlier one. These are, by and large, those who work
but do not live at the Hof.

The services are clearly structured. The Laurentiuskonvent's Office
is made up of introductory responses, hymns, a psalm, Bible-readings
and spontaneous prayer. The hymns come from the Lutheran hymn-
book which is heavily weighted to the Reformation period. Spontaneous prayer is always to the point, with intercession for events
and people close to the community.

Volunteers who participated in the worship had expressed unease
about the structure of it and this had uncovered a latent discontent
in the members of the Laurentiuskonvent itself. 'We are,' said one of
the brothers, 'now more sensitive to the spiritual situation of a young
person living today in modern urban society. We see how impossible
it is for them to integrate themselves into our style of prayer, worship
and intercession.' Accordingly, a number of liturgical experiments
have evolved. Most notable of these are the Sunday morning breakfast
eucharist and the *Shalom*-evening. At the eucharist, which takes
place round the breakfast table, there is as great a degree of participa-
tion as possible. There is no sermon (for Germans, whether Lutheran
or Reformed, this is an important break with the past); everybody
offers their thoughts on a passage of scripture. At the very end after
the bread and wine have been passed from hand to hand the Beati-
tudes are read. There is a peculiar appropriateness about 'Blessed
are the peacemakers'.

Shalom-evenings occur less frequently. While some of the young
adult volunteers find it impossible to attend the explicitly Christian
office, all enjoy the *Shalom*-evenings which make no assumptions
about their beliefs. But these evenings have developed their own
ritual. Songs are sung and bread and cheese, with wine, are shared
among all sitting in a circle.

In the material which the Laurentiuskonvent gathered for the
Shalom-Forum at the 1973 Kirchentag was written a piece which
may serve as a summary of the 'vocation of *Shalom*'.

> Man does not live by bread alone . . .
> but by belonging to a closely knit,
> caring community of brothers and
> fellow humans,
>
> by a practical, selfless commitment
> to peace, justice and the salvation

of this world—a commitment which
sets him free from anxiety for himself.

by anticipating in carefree celebration
the certainty and joy of the eternal
Shalom in the coming kingdom of God.

Although the Laurentiuskonvent has a printed 'Rule' more is said
in it about God and his dealings with men than about rules, structures and forms. These exist, but they must always remain provisional,
justifying themselves only by their continued appropriateness. The
community is ambivalent to its rules; it finds that it needs them as
guidelines but also that rules need continual adaptation to what is
actually happening in their lives.

It sees the value of guidelines primarily as giving a security and
certainty within which it can experiment. It is always wishing to
explore what it means to live Christ's teaching in every sphere of life.
And it is a community which changes its work and the practical
application of its ideals as a result of this wish to explore. The
Laurentiuskonvent has found no model on which to base its combination of families and celibates within one life-committed community, and guidelines, even if continually being altered, provide an
alternative point of reference.

The Laurentiuskonvent's hard-pressed predecessors at Finkenwalde would have approved of the existence of even provisional
rules and forms for the community. They would also have been in
sympathy with the Laurentiuskonvent's disciplined approach to
worship and the extent to which everyday life is shared. However the
Finkenwalde model is not necessarily one for our time. The Laurentiuskonvent responds to the contemporary situation as it believes the
gospel enjoins *now*, as the Confessing Church did in the thirties.
Today the Laurentiuskonvent believes its work must be for peace in
this world 'whether that peace is endangered by class-conflict, the
gap between rich and poor nations or by personal problems'.

Laurentiuskonvent is not a community of the young. It is a community of older people confident enough to have made a life-
commitment to each other. There are many ways in which the
Laurentiuskonvent presents useful contrasts to the other four communities, and these will be explored in chapter 9.

4

The Greenbus Community
Glastonbury

Glastonbury is a small town of just over 6,000 inhabitants in central Somerset. The very low-lying land around the town (known as the Vale of Avalon) is completely dominated by the Glastonbury Tor which rises to 520 feet behind the houses. Glastonbury has rich and plentiful associations with the distant past – and with early Christianity and the Arthurian legends in particular.[1] Joseph of Arimathea, the man who buried Christ after the crucifixion according to all the gospel accounts, came to Britain (the legend goes) bringing the chalice used by Christ at the Last Supper. Joseph is said to have settled then in Glastonbury. When, on arriving at Glastonbury in AD 658, the Saxons found a wattle church of whose origin no native was sure, it was Joseph's name which was soon attached to it.

Arthur's assocation with Glastonbury is just as legendary. Though nobody has proved that he was ever there he has long been linked with the Vale of Avalon and with the Glastonbury Tor. By the twelfth century the Benedictine monks at Glastonbury could be believed when they claimed to have found his tomb and that of his queen, Guinevere, inside their abbey.

Arthur and Joseph of Arimathea are powerful symbols in today's Glastonbury. The stately ruined abbey is another potent symbol and the focus of annual pilgrimages by Roman Catholics and Anglicans. Most vital of all the Glastonbury symbols to many is the Tor. The tourists come in their thousands during the summer, mainly to the abbey but also to the Tor, the Chalice Well and St John's churchyard. The Chalice Well is where Joseph is said to have hidden the chalice from the Last Supper in the ground, thereby causing a well to spring. The attraction of the churchyard is a specimen of the Glastonbury thorn which flowers in January. This is said to be the result of Joseph sticking his staff in the ground on arriving in Glastonbury.

Recently many, mainly young, have been to Glastonbury as part of a spiritual search. Some have found that the place has 'good vibes' and have settled there in caravans and even in council houses. Others return each summer. One finds in Glastonbury a swirling chaos of belief. There is, as someone said to me, 'no belief held by someone in Timbuktoo which is not shared by someone in Glastonbury'.[2]

At first the young seekers were welcomed by sympathizers already living in the town. But as the reputation of Glastonbury as a Mecca of the young grew, others arrived for whom a spiritual search was not the prime aim. This was particularly as a result of the Glastonbury Fayre, a free pop festival in 1971 which brought thousands to the Glastonbury area. Most of the townspeople grew increasingly hostile. The young, transient and settlers, took on a stereotype. There was much righteous disapproval of the drawing of Social Security payments, and many regarded the newcomers as thieving and violent. The natives and the bewildered local authority, believing that the youthful invasion represented a threat to the tourist trade, vented their wrath on those who had settled. Those in caravans presented a sitting target.[3] Notices appeared in pubs and cafés, announcing 'No hippies served'. Thus the label 'hippy' was attached and the stereotype of the young was fixed.

There is a dearth of suitable accommodation for the penurious young, although there have been short-lived attempts to open a youth hostel. Many of those passing through are on their own sort of pilgrimage to their holy places of the West Country – Stonehenge, St Ives and St Michael's Mount as well as Glastonbury – and are equipped to rough it. In 1972 the Greenbus camp community began, welcoming throughout the summer all who were prepared to rough it, but wanted a tent over their heads. The name, incidentally, originated from the community leader's van, which unknown to the baptizer, had recently been painted brown and yellow. It has now been sold and is powder blue!

Greenbus was the vision of Jim Nagel, a young Canadian of Mennonite origin. He had been camping himself in Glastonbury for a summer and was much impressed both by the aura of the place and the needs of the young pilgrims who visited the town. Each year since others have come to the cluster of brightly-coloured tents which make up the Greenbus community. Some return each year; others stay, perhaps the whole summer, and then lose touch. There are perhaps a hundred or more short-term visitors who stay in the community each summer for one night or more. Greenbus is well supported by older friends who live nearby and a continuous flow of ideas is maintained.

The hope is that soon the right people and the right amount of money will have emerged and a permanent community will grow out of Greenbus, finding some land to farm near Glastonbury.

The Greenbus community includes both long- and short-term members and consists of different people at different times, a microcosm of the Glastonbury scene. Many stay for only one night, others never intended to stay any longer but do. On average there are about twenty-five campers each night, but numbers have reached a hundred, for example at the 1974 summer solstice. The summer solstice always draws a variety of people to Glastonbury. From the Tor they greet this time when the sun enters the constellation Cancer, on or about 21 June.

Those who stay at Greenbus are of widely different backgrounds. Jim trained as a journalist but does not at present practise his trade. In summer most of his time is spent at the camp; in winter he works to raise money for it and travels, particularly to Taizé, which has inspired much of what happens at Greenbus.[4] Of the others who committed themselves to the camp for the summer of 1974 few had permanent jobs or their own homes. Some had been part of Greenbus before. These included a chef and a student of classics, as well as a young mother and her eight-year-old daughter. Others were at Greenbus for the first time. One of these was an American girl over here for the summer and usually a free-school teacher, who had, like others, stumbled on Greenbus by accident. Some had sought out Glastonbury because they were interested in its legends and religious significance. Others were simply wandering without any particular aim.

Peter was nineteen. In three years of wandering, squatting and searching he had been to Glastonbury many times but never before to Greenbus. Although highly intelligent and articulate he had never stayed in an educational institution long enough to acquire even 'O' levels. He had experimented with hallucinatory drugs and the Divine Light Mission, but was not addicted to either.[5] His thin drained face was pale. Peter is emphatic in calling himself a Christian and wears a cross. The cross bears the wording of the coffin, allegedly that of

Arthur, dug up by the Glastonbury monks in the twelfth century. *'Hic jacet sepultus inclytus rex Arthurus in insula Avallonia.'* 'Here in the island of Avalon lies buried the famous king Arthur.' Quite apart from the grave itself the inscription is of doubtful authenticity. Nevertheless it is a symbol with great significance in Glaston-bury.

Peter is one of those at the centre of the Greenbus community; one of those referred to as 'the Family'. The Family is a group of people round Jim who in effect take responsibility for the running of the camp. They are not chosen; they simply emerge, commit them-selves to the aims of Greenbus and remain. There are no apparent conditions for membership of the Family and members are not always the same. This reflects a genuine openness and lack of defini-tion within the community.

Openness and lack of definition permeate the Glastonbury scene. They lead to uncertainty and to stereotypes. The 'No hippies served' notices make everyone who is the least bit unconventional ask himself 'Will I be refused service?'. Who after all calls himself a hippy? But when you see these notices in virtually every pub or café, and have perhaps been refused service in one you might begin to identify yourself as a 'hippy' (or 'freak' to use the Glastonbury terminology) and begin to act as the stereotype freak. In this way the town becomes divided into 'freaks' and 'straights', and some of the 'freaks' begin actually to behave like the 'dishonest, dirty, smelly, drug-addicted, promiscuous hippies' about whom the 'straights' have learnt from the sensationalist media.[6] At Greenbus too the community is unsure if they are 'freaks' or not. The town would label them as such. And there too the stereotypes are adopted. Sometimes some of the tran-sient members of the community take on the 'freak' stereotype, and rile at what they see as the 'structure' of Greenbus. Structure there is, but it is minimal. Jim and the Family, since they do not entirely reject organization and structure, as do the stereotyped 'freaks', are forced by the rebels into the unwelcome role of the 'straight' Estab-lishment. And so sometimes the camp has divided down these lines. The Family officially makes it known that anybody present in the camp at any one time is equally a member of the community but when rebellion occurs the Family involuntarily closes ranks against the rebels, and in the circumstances it is difficult 'to have an open door to whomever', which is one of the purposes of the camp.[7]

At one point during 1974 the exhausted Family shut their gate and went into retreat for a week, hoping that those who could not accept

their mode of community life would leave. Fortunately the Windsor
Free Festival was about to start and the dissenters departed.

Though those who join Greenbus are predominantly young adults
between sixteen and thirty (most older travellers and tourists prefer
less spartan accommodation) older people join and are welcomed
from time to time. They too have some interest in the religious
significance of Glastonbury. While I was there a man with long grey
hair, sandals, much experience of India and an 'Oxford' accent
joined the camp for a night. Another, who was working as a nurse in
a Devon psychiatric hospital appeared during his 'off' days. He
preferred to be in Glastonbury than with his family, who, he said,
did not share his interest in a 'Christian search'. And a senior teacher
from East Anglia has been at the camp on two occasions for extended
periods.

The aims of Greenbus are 'to learn to live together, work together,
and to pray together – whatever that means – and to have an open
door to whomever'. To some extent they fulfil all of these aims. But
they are always self-critical and in 1974 there was much discussion of
what more the community could do together. This was in anticipa-
tion of the time when, some of them hope, they will own a farm and
will have to work together on it. In the spring before the 1974 summer
camp began there were ambitious plans to make a garden out of a
corner of the field in which they were to camp, to keep chickens and
even to harness solar energy in order to heat water. Only the garden
materialized, producing a prodigious crop mainly of lettuces. Jim
said that so much of what had been dreamt of was impossible because
'we sat around yapping and continually trying to relate to new
guests who came to us without any particular sense of purpose'. The
springtime plans were in a way 'symbolic of the alternative society',
but they would have required consistent effort from all the campers.
And that was impossible with all the Family occupied in keeping 'an
open door to whomever'.

Many felt a restlessness through doing no regular physical work
with the others around them; and more and more members of the
community during 1974 were finding unskilled jobs in the Glastonbury area. A useful by-product of this was cash for the community's
hard-pressed kitty. But there was in fact much work to be done at the
camp. Apart from cooking for up to twenty-five and keeping the
communal tent clean, milk and water had to be fetched from the
farm. There was no running water at the camp. Somebody kept an

eye on the garden, and on the primitive trenches which were the camp's only toilet facilities. Naomi, who was eight, had to be taken to and collected from school every day and others, as well as her mother, took responsibility for this.

Outside the confines of the community Greenbus took on part responsibility in 1974 for the Information Centre in Glastonbury. A member of the camp staffed it each afternoon. Seen by some as a 'bridge between "freaks" and "straights" ', the Information Centre is an unofficial enterprise able to help visitors with accommodation problems, provide material on the Glastonbury legends and local spiritual happenings and try to meet the hundred other needs of young wanderers.

During the summer of 1974 Jim was talking of plans for an expansion of the Information Centre work. Greenbus, he thought, might be able to operate a shop which could combine under one roof activities close to the heart of many at the camp – a coffee house, a recycling centre, a wall-poster community newspaper and so on. Always Greenbus aims to be open to those in need while living by ecological principles.

When trying to understand the work a community does it is easy enough to list its overt activities but much more difficult to describe its less tangible work. The most important function of the Greenbus camp is to keep its door ever open. It is the only place in Glastonbury where penniless wanderers can be received; it is also a place (and this is less tangible) where those wanderers or seekers who need support can find it. Greenbus provides security to many rootless people. One member who was in court for jumping bail while on remand for a petty offence told the magistrate about Greenbus and was given a discharge conditional on his remaining at the camp. Another member, who was very quiet until he roared back after closing-time one night and shouted till 4 a.m. was able to overcome his alcoholic craving on other evenings by sitting with others round the camp-fire. Nobody suggested he be asked to leave; the only consequence of the disturbance was that prayers were at 9 instead of 7 the following morning.

Glastonbury is full of young adults and others who are not prepared to fit comfortably into a niche in what they regard as conventional society. Some find it hard to maintain this sort of unconventional stance. By and large these are the ones whom Greenbus most supports, a support given chiefly by the invisible structure of the community, and by the fact that there exists a place where there are sympathetic, equally-unconventional people who will be there and prepared to listen.

Nobody is encouraged to think of his tent as exclusively for his own use. Some tents have been given to the camp and are generally available. To those who come to Glastonbury with only a sleeping bag Greenbus is attractive since it offers tent-space. One very large military tent was loaned to the camp in 1974 by Christian Action and that housed the kitchen as well as providing space for up to twenty to sleep.

Everybody eats communally as far as possible although some who were going to work had to leave before the 7.30 a.m. breakfast. Meals are cooked by anybody who feels moved, though in spite of the fact that girls were very much in a minority and also of there being two men with experience as chefs in the camp, the cooks were more often than not female. 'Nibbling' food other than what was prepared was frowned upon. Breakfast and supper are eaten in the camp and a picnic lunch is eaten in the grounds of the ruined abbey. As well as the regular office before each meal a simple grace is said on behalf of the company, expressing appreciation and gratitude for the food, the weather, the day. At this point all present are joined by the physical link of holding hands.

Meals are vegetarian and this is taken for granted. Those who are looking towards a permanent community want to adjust their diet to include so far as possible those foods they can grow and produce themselves. Many of the community were vegetarian before they came to the camp. They also believe that a vegetarian diet of dairy foods, vegetables, fruit and nuts avoids the exploitation of animals and leads to simple and healthy living. In addition the community eats only the brown varieties of rice, bread and sugar, since they prefer foods as near to their natural state as possible. While I was there there was a move to ban sugar altogether from their diet on the grounds that it was unhealthy. This was unsuccessful. Butter, however, was used as little as possible because it was considered both unhealthy and a luxury.

Vegetarianism is linked with Greenbus' attempt to live as simply as possible. Jim writes: 'We are trying to learn to do without money – to cut expenses to the minimum and less, by making it ourselves, making do or doing without – pretending the depression is already upon us and learning to Enjoy it.' An inalienable part of their living simply is ecological awareness. Compost is scrupulously kept and nurtured for the lettuces, waste is deplored and foods grown without artificial fertilizers are eaten as far as possible. Now that the green bus has been sold the community has no mechanized transport.

Simple living is not only a matter of principle but is also the result of necessity. Many who come to the camp have no money. No pressure is put on those who have no money to contribute to the 'kitty', which covers all expenses. In 1974 the Family were expected to contribute £3 per week; others did so too. This was enough to cover those (about six while I was there) who were not contributing. In addition a Canadian church had recently given Greenbus £75. Whether the free facilities of the camp are 'misused' by those who contribute nothing is for the community itself to say. Mutterings were occasionally heard that a limit should be put on the stay of non-contributors.

The farmer also levied 10p per person per night for camping in his field and the camp was responsible for collecting this sum.

The rhythm of camp life is maintained each day with prayers before each meal, at 7 a.m. and 1 p.m. and 7 p.m. The office of the Society of St Francis (the Anglican Franciscans) is used. This contains the traditional elements of responses, psalm said antiphonally, readings from Old and New Testaments and (sometimes) canticles and is based on mattins and evensong as used in the Church of England. There is also an extended time of silence for private thought and prayer, usually broken by somebody praying aloud. But the order of worship is not fixed. During part of the summer of 1974 the community stopped saying the Franciscan office in the evening and replaced it, Quaker-style, only with silence which people could interrupt if they had something to contribute to the meditations of their fellows.

The office was the centre of the life of the Family. Most of them attended, even if not always three times a day and even if not calling themselves Christians. There were others there too on most occasions. The office was always said outside if possible; if at the camp, sitting overlooking the Vale of Avalon – a view which certainly concentrates the mind. The lunchtime office was said in the abbey grounds, on the site of the first Glastonbury church with which Joseph of Arimathea is associated, or if it was wet, in the crypt dedicated to him. The lunchtime prayers had been kept up through the winter of 1973/4 even though Greenbus had dispersed – an almost tangible link with the early Christians at Glastonbury.

At the end of this lunchtime office the 'four sentences' announced at Taizé as the first message of the preparation for the Council of Youth were said as a prayer:[8]

> O Risen Christ, come and quicken a festival in the innermost heart of man. Prepare for us a springtime of the church, a church devoid of means of power, ready to share with all, a place of visible communion for all humanity. Give us enough imagination and courage to open up a path of reconciliation. O Risen Christ, prepare us to give our lives so that man be no longer victim of man.

These words, said at one of England's oldest Christian sites, symbolize the bringing together of contemporary expressions of the Christian hope and the rich tradition of two thousand years of Christianity. Occasionally, passing tourists join these lunchtime orisons. One such (a young American girl) deeply affected after sharing the office said, 'I knew I must have come to Glastonbury for some reason.'

Greenbus is acknowledged to have a Christian identity. This reputation has not been won by aggressiveness, but by a quiet presence in Glastonbury. The rhythm of daily life is set by the pattern of Christian worship and also by the meals. It seems also that Christian belief has an integrating function for the community. It provides a system of meaning in the lives of some individuals at the camp and since these individuals are by and large the leaders of the community Christianity integrates the life of the camp. It also provides the community with an ideal against which to test itself. Yet at the same time a majority of the campers do not share many of the widely-held assumptions of Christian belief and the community's worship is a focus not only for the practising Christians in the camp, but also for others who would not call themselves Christian. This is particularly true of the Family, who, although both Christian and non-Christian, all join the worship. And they do so for perhaps two reasons.

First, by being members of the Family they associate themselves with the Christian basis of the camp and the activities and daily rhythm of the community; these are explicitly Christian. The Christian view of reality is endorsed at Greenbus and it is the only coherent view of reality which is available. Those who experience the numinous at Glastonbury can express their experience in terms of this available view of reality and, indeed, seem happy to do so. In the fluidity of their religious expression they do not expect to do justice to the claims of Christian doctrine.

A second reason for non-Christians joining the worship at Greenbus is this. The office is obviously relevant to the life at Greenbus.
The *Venite Adoremus* of the morning office and other psalms and
biblical passages written for and in a rural society have a clear
relevance when one is sitting on the slopes of the Tor facing Wells
Cathedral or in the grounds of Glastonbury Abbey. The wonder of
creation as expressed in, say, the psalms is readily understood by a
group of people longing to live off the land. So the Family finds itself
able to express its togetherness in terms of Christianity, even when
not all of them call themselves Christian.

Sometimes, when there has been tension in the camp and the
Family has become isolated, Christianity has all too easily become
the sign of division, although 'the offence of the cross', as Jim put it
quoting St Paul, had apparently nothing to do with the point at
issue. The Family have been told that as Christians they should do
this, or do that, and that when not all of them are Christian. Yet this
sort of attitude does not imply any battle of religions. The field of
religious belief at Glastonbury is too diversified for that.

Something has already been said about the Glastonbury legends.
There are many beliefs peculiar to Glastonbury, some connected
with the legends, others not. In any case many at Glastonbury,
natives and visitors, hold beliefs which in most other parts of the
British Isles would strike no chords. But there is no coherent Glastonbury belief-system or theology. An individual builds up his beliefs
from the legends about Arthur or Joseph of Arimathea; or even from
the mythical characters of Tolkien. He may hold beliefs about the
existence of ley-lines and power-points[9] and the importance of the
stars under which people are born. Some Christians and some non-
Christians alike at Greenbus talked approvingly of all these beliefs,
however, and acted as if they were true. On a day, for example, in
which tension had arisen in the camp one of those most deeply
involved and a Christian since being converted in the camp the
previous year, explained that the tensions were due to the fact that
we were on a ley-line. Almost all in the camp also knew something
about astrology and talked of characteristics likely to be exhibited
by those born under Capricorn, Cancer and other stars. I often
heard people say that they 'got on well with Capricorns' (for example).

The Glastonbury legends also play a significant part in the life of
the camp. The lunchtime prayers in the Abbey are deliberately linked
with Joseph.[10] He and Arthur are special figures whose association
with Glastonbury is unquestionable. They, and particularly Arthur,

have become in Glastonbury symbols of the New Age, which many believe is dawning.[11] In spite of an entrance fee nearly half the camp attended a lecture in summer 1974 on 'The Search for King Arthur' organized by the Aquarian Centre and given by Geoffrey Ashe, author of books on Arthur and Glastonbury. Ashe said that 'in whatever sense we mean it' Arthur will return. This might, he said, be in the form of an 'Arthur-type figure' who would actually be reincarnated with the characteristics of Arthur, or it might be simply that the characteristics associated with Arthur (spirituality, artistic gifts and living in tune with nature) would become dominant in the nation as a whole and the New Age be ushered in.

In Glastonbury one lives so much amongst these beliefs and the features of the countryside and town which seem to confirm them that they become almost credible. The context makes them credible. If an openness to them is already present in an individual and if they are held already by people who look, behave and talk in the same way as he does, and with whom he is living, then it takes little for him to take them as his own. This applies as much to Christianity at Glastonbury as to these other beliefs which are peculiar to Glastonbury.

In spite of there being this unusual supplement to Christian belief at Greenbus many of the campers are active in the life of the local parish church, attending services, singing in the choir and so on. The vicar of Glastonbury has celebrated the eucharist at the camp. And the Bishop of Bath and Wells, in whose diocese this is, has twice been asked for, and has given, his blessing to the camp, and any advice he wished to proffer. But significantly most campers reacted with distaste to the traditional Anglican pilgrimage to Glastonbury in which the bishop is glorified to a degree also distasteful to many in the Church of England.

The world of the monastic orders is part of Greenbus' life and ideals. In a purely physical sense the ruined Benedictine abbey is at the centre of Glastonbury. For Greenbus the abbey is also at the centre of their inspiration. The community says its midday office there every day, using the office not of the Benedictines but of the Anglican Franciscans. Jim has indeed made a personal link with the Society of St Francis. In addition a member of the Community of the Resurrection has spent a lot of time with Greenbus.

Links with the monastic world are more than personal. The daily rhythm of the camp community is like that of a monastic community in its emphasis on worship and meals as the times at which the community comes together.

Many campers, whether Christian or not, are familiar with the life and ideals of those religious orders (including the Community of the Resurrection and the Society of St Francis) which are outward-looking. Many have stayed in monasteries and convents; indeed one camper could compile a directory of monastic institutions and their attractions for the wanderer. And another expressed real admiration for the Franciscans as they hitch-hike from place to place with the minimum of possessions. Three who came to the camp for a couple of nights won high praise. They were described as 'freaky'.

As an ideal for the future too the image of an abbey draws the Family on. Their permanent community will not, it is true, bear much similarity to the monied magnificence of the medieval Glastonbury Abbey. Rather it will be like the faltering efforts of the earlier Christians in a Britain largely hostile to the 'offence of the cross'. The focus of the new community will be on the land and it will try to be self-supporting. Jim associates himself with the ideal of St Bernard, founder of the Cistercian order, that his community should cultivate its own land by its own labour for its own use.

Towards the end of the 1974 camp Greenbus celebrated two events; the feast of St Bernard (20 August) and the opening of the Council of Youth at Taizé (30 August), symbolizing the fact that its way forward needs both the example of the past and the challenge of the present.

5

The Cinisello Community
Milan, Italy

Cinisello is a working-class suburb of Milan. If the name is familiar to anyone outside Italy it is probably because a commune in this suburb has gained for itself a far-flung reputation.

The Cinisello Commune is a largely Protestant group in an over-whelmingly Catholic land. I found it impossible to see the community in isolation; it is essential to look at the position of the Protestants as a whole, their politics and their attitude to the Catholic establish-ment represented not only by the hierarchy but also by the Christian Democrat party.

The Protestant churches in Italy are extremely small. The three chief ones (Waldensian, Methodist, Baptist) have a total membership of about 50,000. Even with Pentecostalists and Adventists the total number of Protestants is less than 1 % of the Italian population. The Waldensian Church, although claiming to be the oldest Protestant church—it is certainly medieval—allied itself with the Calvinists in the sixteenth century and since then has considered itself Reformed. It suffered terribly from Catholic-sponsored persecutions. This has not been forgotten and the present Protestant suspicion of the Catholic hierarchy is, I was told, in part due to the earlier perse-cutions.

All three Protestant churches have close ties and amicable arrange-ments about the use of their buildings. In addition youth work is now carried out ecumenically under the auspices of FGEI (Italian Protestant Youth Federation).

Many Protestants are doubtful both about the Catholic hierarchy's influence in the state and about the practice it encourages. While, for example, the Vatican and the Christian Democrats oppose the possi-bility of divorce in Italy, Protestants are generally in favour of allowing it. The Waldensian publishing house has even published a booklet explaining that while Christians should live themselves according to Christ's teaching on divorce they have no right to write this into the laws of the state. Again, a number of Protestants have been attacking what they claim to be the superstitious element in Catholic practice, and particularly the celebration of the festivals of saints. A broadsheet distributed in a parish in Turin, which was celebrating the obscure St Rita, used Isaiah 1.12–17 ('Your new moons and your appointed feasts my soul hates . . .; seek justice, correct oppression, defend the fatherless, plead for the widow.') to suggest that the pursuit of justice was more important for the Christian than the celebration of saints' days; and Matthew 21.12–14 (the throwing of the money-changers out of the temple) to attack the commercialism of festivals.

These Protestant positions are shared by *Cattolici del Dissenso* (dissenting Catholics), Catholics who are still very much Christian but out of sympathy with their hierarchy. In the 1974 referendum on divorce these voted against the hierarchy for the possibility of divorce in Italy. They also tend to vote for, or be active in, parties of the Italian left. One much-noted development among such Catholics has been the formation of *communita di base*. These are communities of Christians (often living together) engaged in mainly social and political work in working-class areas. Most are led by priests and have an uneasy relationship with the hierarchy, who are apparently suspicious of the role played by priests in these communities.[1]

Attitudes to the Catholic Church and political standpoints are inextricably bound up in Italy. The Protestants are not simply critical of the Catholic establishment; they are also by and large left-wing. Although perhaps a majority of Italian Protestants vote for the Socialist party some vote for or are active in the powerful Communist party. In one Waldensian parish in Southern Italy the entire congregation votes Communist. That parish has carefully thought out its position. One of its peasant members said, addressing a regional Communist gathering, that Jesus Christ came into the world to preach equality and that the poorest and marginals listened to him. The church later became allied with the most dehumanized and oppressive power. 'We Protestants intend to join again the movement begun by Jesus.'[2] Although this parish is 'exceptional' in the Waldensian Church and although it has only recently experienced this development the links between Protestantism and the Italian left are well established.

The Protestant Youth Federation (FGEI) is perhaps unique in Western Europe in that it is the only official church youth organization which has, as it claims, 'chosen to work and fight side by side with the working classes'. In other countries, FGEI claims, it is not the entire youth movement of a church but only small marginal Christian groups which have made such a choice.

The political interests of FGEI go back to 1968 the year of student turmoil in Paris. The upheavals of that year affected Italy almost as much as France. The Protestant youth of Italy, as many others all over the world, became aware that many of their contemporaries were deeply influenced by the writings of Karl Marx, and faced the fact that this had implications for themselves and for the capitalist society in which they lived. A radical shift occurred during the following year, and when the Federation was formed from the three separate youth organizations of the Waldensian, Methodist and Baptist churches, it had, it now says, made a Marxist choice. But their Protestant roots take them at the same time back to the Bible. Their chaplains encourage them in this combination of Marx and holy scripture, but one of them told me that he finds his members more politically than theologically aware.

The 1971 FGEI Congress spelt out in a final document the position of the Federation. This amply illustrates current thinking among Protestant young people. And because most of the Cinisello Commune members are past or present members of FGEI it tells us something about the commune.

(a) Today's most fundamental problems are the confession of faith and a genuine anti-capitalist involvement.

(b) Young Italian Protestants must analyse the relation between classes and act as a 'clarifying presence' among the proletariat.

(c) For this Marxist theory represents the most adequate instrument.

(d) Faith does not exhaust itself in the struggle for socialism but faith can be enriched by social involvement.

(e) The Bible must be read and a dialectical relationship maintained between word and practice.[3]

The number of members in FGEI groups is small, perhaps fifteen in each, and their influence on Italian life limited. Their influence on the Protestant churches, however, is enormous, and young Protestants maintain a rare closeness with their elders. There is no question of whether to work within or outside the institutional church. That question is almost irrelevant. For Protestant churches in Italy are not 'established', furthermore they have no links with the 'Establishment'. They have always been tiny minorities and have nothing to lose in terms of social status or financial backing if their youth make revolutionary statements. Besides, and the implications are hard for a Briton to appreciate, the extreme left, in the shape of the Communists, with well over a quarter of the seats in the lower house of the Italian parliament is not under the beds, but in them, and respectable. The 1975 regional elections brought further gains to the Italian Communist Party.

Cinisello (the place) is a large suburb of Milan, six miles from the city centre. The development of Cinisello might also have been the development of many other towns in Western Europe which happen to be situated near expanding industrial centres. In 1936 Cinisello was a mainly agricultural centre with a population of about 12,000. In 1974 it was heavily industrial with a population of about 100,000. Roughly half of those who work are employed outside the municipality. There is a high rate of unemployment. The industrial jobs available are in small concerns or in the factories of the multinationals nearby, including Pirelli, Alfa Romeo, IBM and Philips. Most inhabitants live in box-like, unexciting and haphazardly-planned blocks of flats. There is very little green to be seen even in the spring around these blocks.

A large proportion of the population increase in Cinisello is due to immigration from the south of Italy where jobs are scarce and many live in extreme poverty. When the immigrants arrive their standard of living may rise (if they have found a job) but other factors which they have not expected cause them problems. First, there are the problems associated with housing; land speculation, unoccupied houses and little central planning to curb *laissez-faire* building. In addition Cinisello has lost the community feeling of a small town. Then there are also the problems which are perhaps particularly acute for a southern Italian moving to the north. ('A peasant from Sicily who becomes a factory worker in Cinisello gets a greater culture shock than a Milanese worker who moves to London,' said the Waldensian pastor in Cinisello.) The Sicilian peasant has left behind the deep roots he had in his rural community and a morality which was almost universally accepted. In the north he finds that this morality is no longer confirmed by his neighbours, or even his children. The children of immigrants often develop a different morality from that of their parents in matters of sex and respect for the property of other people. The parents often do not understand that it is their very move from south to north, from peasant to worker, which has upset their children's *mores*, and think that they can 'cure' their children by sending them out to work earlier than is strictly legal and then by encouraging them to work as long hours as possible to keep them out of trouble. This only creates further problems and leads to under-payment of the under-age children.

Cinisello has had a left-wing (Socialist and Communist) town council since 1946. The Communist party has a strong working class base here and the leaning to the parties on the left is shown by any election result. Even in the divorce referendum it was obvious. While the national result was 59%–41% in favour of permitting divorce Cinisello's result was 77%–23%. The walls of the town were decorated with political graffiti to an extent seen in Britain only around universities and in Northern Ireland. Passers-by were urged to show their solidarity with Vietnam, the IRA and Frelimo, were informed about 'provocation' against squatting families in Cinisello who had recently been evicted, and treated to diatribes against the Neo-Fascist party.

It is in this highly politicized area that the commune also known as Cinisello lives and works. The commune lives in one of the ordinary, box-like blocks of flats. In front of the block is waste-land where children play; behind is a development site. There are twenty-six members, including three families with seven children between them. Apart from those with children there are also two more married couples in the commune. Since the commune began in 1968 there have been some changes of membership and in 1974 there were in total seven members more than in 1968. The occupations of the group are diverse. Some are teachers, some workers, one a student. One is an IBM technician, one a salesman, one a bookseller. Originally the group was entirely Protestant. Now of the nineteen adult members eleven identify themselves as Protestant, four as Catholics and four as atheists. The commune, however, is still widely thought of as a Protestant group. All members are Italian except for one American volunteer sent to Cinisello for two years by a church volunteer agency. Only the six parents are over thirty and Cinisello is mainly a young adult group.

The original group came together in the form of a community in 1968. Many had known each other for some time; the Protestant world in Italy is small. But none then was active in Cinisello. They joined the Waldensian pastor responsible for the north Milanese suburbs, and his family, who had been sent to Cinisello with an open brief two years earlier. The group wanted to be among the working class and they decided to start an evening school for young workers. But the question immediately arises: 'Why form a community?'

When the Cinisello group was planning its future in 1968 it had the example of other Italian Protestant communities before it. The Agape community had been started in the Italian Alps in 1951 and another at Riesi, in Sicily, some time later. The Cinisello pastor and his family had shared their lives with another family before this venture. Family communitarianism, though perhaps numerically infrequent, is certainly more central to the experience of Italy's Protestant churches than it is to those of Britain.

For the founding of Cinisello there were perhaps two reasons above all. The community speaks of the need to overcome 'the feeling of isolation and the stifling atmosphere' of a nuclear family, which they consider 'a typical product of a bourgeois society'. Secondly from the start the group was convinced that although largely middle class itself, it had come to work among the Cinisello working class and could work effectively only by living under the same conditions as the locals. Although communal living is no more frequent among the Italian working class than among the British working class, the thinking appears to be that isolated middle-class families can come closest to working-class solidarity by living communally.

For these reasons the community was formed. It was 'never considered as an end in itself; it had to be an instrument of common activity, the school and social involvement'. From the beginning others helped in the running of the school; there was no exclusiveness, either deliberate or accidental, about the commune. The numbers of helpers and friends who give support by dropping in, sharing the problems of the school and so on, is now almost eighty. Many of these are former students of the school. 'The school stopped us becoming exclusive,' says Giorgio Bouchard, the Waldensian pastor and *de facto* leader of the commune 'During the first two or three years the school was unsure of success and all the work of the commune was for the school. We had to be outward-looking.' 'Nor', writes his wife, 'did we hold long theoretical debates about the aims of a "commune" in our society. We were too busy with the practical work at our school to have much time for debating.'

The twenty-six members of the commune live for the most part in one large block, in different flats on three floors. One couple with their child live in the next block and one newly-married couple, who lived in the block as single people, have moved out to a neighbouring suburb. Their own opinion is that it is not necessary to live on the spot to be members of the community. They will probably move back into the commune later. By and large each family has a flat to itself and the single people live in two flats which have been joined. One, however, lives with one of the families. The community rents the whole of the fourth floor of the block and the three flats there are interconnected. The common rooms – kitchen and large open-plan room which is dining and sitting/discussion room in one – are there. So is the office of the secretary, who is a member of the commune. The pastor's family has less privacy than the other families and couples because their flat is next to the common rooms. The three children of this family are happy with the present arrangement but they see less of their busy father than they would in a normal family. The father says, 'When they do have their *pappa* they get concentrated attention because a commune cannot be an evasion of parental responsibility.'

So, whatever the commune writes about nuclear families, there is no attempt to weaken the links between parents and children.

In the physical organization of the flats there is a great deal of autonomy for the commune's members. But most meals are taken together, and the children eat with the adults. Kitchen duties are performed according to a rota, which includes both male and female members of the community. There is a 'signing-up' system for each meal and catering is done on the basis of the number who express their intention in advance to eat. It is not expected that every person will attend every meal. Guests are frequent, and, as is the Italian custom, meals are prolonged with conversation. At Cinisello such conversation is, more often than not, political. During the week some go off to teach in the school after the evening meal but local young adults drop in and discussions and chats will continue in the common room, sometimes all night.

Since the early days there has been a major change in the composition of the community. The community has always had an 'experimental character'. But it was a challenge to its non-exclusiveness and 'experimental character' when at the beginning of 1972 some four unmarried workers, who had no church affiliation but who were already friends of the commune and lived locally, wanted to become members. This, says Giorgio, was a turning point. 'If we had not accepted them, on the grounds that they had no church, we would have made a mistake.' He would now like more workers to become full members. The class mix has brought a development of 'personal solidarity between the middle- and working-class members of the commune'. The effect of the workers has been felt particularly in the financial arrangements of the commune.

These arrangements changed in February 1974 when a more equitable system of income sharing was adopted, after much heart-searching. On the initiative of the new worker members of the commune, the original system, by which each family or individual in the commune paid a fixed sum towards the rent of the common rooms and for each meal taken, was amended. The new system basically introduces the principle that those who earn more should pay more; sacrifices are thus demanded of the higher earners. Payment towards the common purse (for meals and rent of the common rooms) is now assessed as a percentage of the individual or family's total income and not as a fixed sum which is the same for all members. Thus a worker earning less will pay less. Families with children do not pay extra for them. This is still far from the total sharing of incomes, but it has been difficult to get this far. However, many feel that 'the extent to which we can give up privileges is a test of our Christian credibility' and 'to do away with private property is the aim we are slowly and freely moving towards'. At present, apart from the articles in the common rooms (books, furniture, office equipment, kitchen gadgets, etc.) nothing is held in common. Each family and many individuals have some consumer goods of their own. In addition, all members contribute towards a third of the cost of running the evening school. The other two-thirds of the cost of the school is found from other sources, notably from Protestant churches outside Italy, through the World Council of Churches.

There is no official leader of the community. The pastor is the nominal director of the school for which the community is responsible, because the state insists that someone should sign certificates and so on. And since the pastor was in Cinisello first and in a sense the community has gathered round him and his family, his standing is considerable. But the commune is 'informal'. Leadership tends to be assumed by those who work hardest for the commune. Organizational problems have tended to devolve on to the pastor and his wife. But during 1973/4 a change in leadership was taking place.

Whereas previously the 'hard workers' were those now over thirty-five now a good half of them are between twenty-two and twenty-eight. This change may prove eventually to be extremely significant, because those within this age group include the non-Protestants who have joined, both Catholic and atheist. Important decisions about the commune and new members are taken by all the members, however. Sometimes applications for membership are refused if the commune thinks the candidate needs too much support. The group says it cannot afford to have dependent people who are joining for the wrong reason.

The evening school is central to the life of the community. Without it, or something like it, the community would have no *raison d'être*. (Originally a kindergarten was considered but rejected on the grounds that it would involve too few people.) And yet, in terms of man-hours, the school is a secondary occupation for most members of the community who teach there only after doing a day's work elsewhere. Those few people who do not teach in the school are all taking 'a strong interest' in it.

The choice of the evening school as the channel of the group's energies in Cinisello depended to some extent on the particular time at which the question arose. The Italian educational system was under fire from many sides in 1967/8 and it was a time when many realized its inadequacies. The influential book *Lettera a Una Professora* came out in 1967.[4] Soon afterwards student rumblings sharpened many criticisms of Italian education.

Other factors also affected the choice of the school as an activity. First the particular people who began the Cinisello group were well-equipped, academically, to run an evening school, being mainly teachers, students and white-collar workers. Secondly, everybody could be involved in the running of the school because a large number of teachers, substitutes and course devisers would be needed. Thirdly, since the town of Cinisello had no evening school and the need for one was clear, an evening school could provide the group with the opportunity it wanted to become part of the local community. The need for an evening school arises because 30% of Cinisello children do not complete their eight years' of compulsory schooling. They leave of their own accord, or because their parents urge them to find a job, or because the school expels them. The children then receive no certificate that they have finished the eight years' schooling and passed the final examination of the junior high school. Thus they are officially ineligible for most jobs since even manual labouring requires a certificate of completion of education. The evening school therefore prepares its students for the junior high school examination.

Since 1970 about twenty pupils (boys and girls) have taken the examination each year. In 1974 there were thirty-one. Of these nineteen gained the grading *Ottimo* (Excellent) and twelve *Distincto* (Very Good). Indeed out of the eighty candidates in the first four years only three failed. The evening course lasts two years and each week one subject is studied without a break for two hours each night. English, Italian, Science, History and Mathematics are taught and space is sometimes found for Art and Geography. The pupils are mostly aged between fifteen and twenty and almost all are the children of southern immigrants. The course is free.

There are many differences from the normal Italian school. First the staff are not all professional teachers. Two-thirds are students, workers, clerks and so on. In addition the teachers cultivate a more informal relationship with their pupils than is normal. All sit round a table, the teacher is addressed by his or her first name, and classes are small. The teaching materials are different from those in ordinary Italian schools. Often they are written specially for the situation of the students. The English course in the first year (before the texts for the examination are tackled in the second year) consists of conversations composed by the American volunteer. The conversation is about Cinisello town and its working young people as well as about England or America. The usual school text book conversations are about middle-class English or American families whose way of life is rather different from that of young people in Cinisello. Cinisello young people find it easier to learn English in lessons which come close to home. Furthermore, by taking every opportunity to relate their studies to their local situation, the teachers hope to raise the awareness of the students about life in Cinisello.

In the second year the school must submit examination texts to the education authorities for their approval. Some of those submitted would never be considered in an ordinary school. For example, for the 'Epic' section of the Italian examination Cinisello submitted George Jackson's *Soledad Brother* instead of the usual Virgil's *Aeneid*. This was eventually accepted since the Education Ministry allows flexible programmes. A school run on similar lines by a FGEI group in Naples submitted for their Italian examination biblical texts (including Isaiah and Psalm 137) and Marx-Engel's *Communist Manifesto* instead of Manzoni, Leopardi and Homer.[5]

During the classes, at least in the first year, the teachers do not restrict themselves to material which would conventionally be covered by their subject. A first year Science lesson I looked in on, for example was discussing the differences between Italian political parties. Some students accustomed to a less generous interpretation of the extent of the subject cannot adjust to this sort of thing. The community has written, 'quite a few (of the students) could not take seriously . . . a Science class where working conditions in factories or occupational diseases were debated, or an Italian class where newspapers and even comic strips were read, a Geography lesson where they studied local problems or listened to a report on a recent trip to China'.

Another difference from ordinary schools is that every six weeks there is a students' assembly, in which the teachers are silent as far as possible and the students discuss their courses. Many students have expressed unease with the interpretation of the subject titles. They have, however, 'tended to keep a passive attitude, asking for explanation about a choice already made by the teacher instead of advancing new proposals or opposing the old ones'.

So what effect does the work of the Cinisello group have as regards its evening school? The primary effect is that the qualifications of the students are improved and they are more likely to find a job. A by-product of the course has often been that the students gain ease in expression and discussion and many go on to become active in trade unions. It is claimed that another by-product of the courses is that when young adults attend every evening five days a week for two years their way of life is affected. The temptations to drink endlessly and steal, which in Cinisello are difficult to resist because of the absence of other entertainment, are greatly reduced.

If it is suggested that what is happening in Cinisello is a teacher-manipulation of a new kind, a teaching style which the students do not appreciate but which the teachers are not prepared to alter, the answer is given that 'the students were conditioned by their former experience in traditional schools'. This parallels a wider debate in which those who take the community's view argue that traditional schooling acts as an agent of social control by inculcating a society's values.[6] Granted, but it could also be argued that the Cinisello school is no less an instrument of social control than a traditional school. The texts and subject matter of the lessons are chosen with the intention of stimulating awareness of what the teachers think to be

important. The students are inculcated with what the teachers consider to be the values and aims of the working class, or rather, what
the teachers consider ought to be those aims and values. To this sort
of criticism the Cinisello group would answer that any educational
process is bound to act as an instrument of social control, and to
counterbalance the influence of bourgeois education they aim to
provide for the youth of Cinisello the materials they need to develop
a working-class consciousness.

Some of the students make friends with the Cinisello group on a
personal level and go upstairs to chat in the community's common
room. Some former students have become teachers in the school;
some have even joined the commune. But it is certainly not the aim
of the school to increase the numbers in the commune. More often,
the members of the group, particularly Giorgio and his wife, are
able to give pastoral help to the young adults, who are not only the
students but also their friends and their friends' friends. The common
room is somewhere to go where there will always be someone to talk
to. The door to the flat with the common room is always open.

Undoubtedly the school has been a successful way of getting inside
the local community. Before long the commune had understood the
seriousness of problems such as the employment situation, the culture
shock for southern immigrants and the exploitation of under-age
workers. This had only been achieved by living on the spot and by
making contacts through the school, establishing a mutual trust with
the youth of the district.

The community has thought hard about its 'witness'. The Walden-
sians are in the Reformed tradition and both they and the Methodists
in the community belong to churches which in Italy have been greatly
influenced by Karl Barth. They start from the belief that they are
saved by God's grace alone, and that 'works' are not instruments to
salvation. Any activity in which they engage, any political stance
they take cannot therefore be a substitute for *preaching* the gospel.
The pastor jokingly tells the atheist and the Catholic members of the
community that the Protestants will try to convert them and indeed
two Catholics became Protestants in 1974. Nevertheless this is
'witness' with qualifications. 'We ought,' writes the community, 'as
believers today to start speaking again [of their faith] only after
living with our fellow creatures in everyday life and after sharing the
contradictions that class struggle forces upon the exploited and after
participating actively in working out a programme aimed at creating

a movement to upset the present power structures of our society.'
These, then, are the qualifications which the community feels must
be placed on its witness. The faith of its members must not be com-
promised but it cannot be maintained as if the local environment did
not exist.

Bible study has been important to the group from the beginning.
At present this is held weekly, though while I was at Cinisello it had
been temporarily suspended because of the divorce referendum campaign in which community members were involved. One of the
commune members also runs a Bible study for other technicians in
his 'shop' at IBM.

There are many ways of reading the Bible. Cinisello distinguishes
between reading it for guidance and reading it to justify a stand
which has already been taken. They hope that they read it for
guidance. The Bible speaks about opposing injustice and oppression
and the Cinisello community consider that it is their reading of the
Bible which has committed them to giving up their careers and
comparatively peaceful lives in Milan to live amidst what they see as
the injustice and oppression of Cinisello. 'But,' says Giorgio, 'we
don't need to *justify* our political commitment from the Bible. We
must have courage to take responsibility for our own actions.
Christianity cannot be tied down to a political programme and God
does not look more favourably on a socialist than on anyone else.'
Giorgio does not therefore see the need to prove that Christ sided
with the political revolutionaries of his time though, he says, such
proof would be interesting.

It is not easy for Italian Protestants to read the Bible with Catholics and atheists. Nor is it easy to worship together. The openness
practised by the community in other fields was difficult to extend to
liturgical activities. Early attempts at a Sunday morning service, with
experimental worship including a eucharist and biblical discussion,
were eventually defeated by the different needs of those taking part.
The commune members were by and large interested in 'profound
study' while outsiders with no previous theological experience found
it meaningless. (The Blackheath commune which existed in South
London between 1969 and 1971, found similarly that their attempts
to study the Bible were defeated by varying degrees of expertise. Very
soon an 'elitist' study group developed for those with degrees in
theology!) At present the Cinisello commune has no worship together. Many attend the Protestant churches and some of the children
go to Sunday School. Two of the Catholics still attend Mass occa-

sionally. The pastor has in any case many liturgical duties among his scattered congregation in the northern suburbs of Milan.

Although all the members of the commune are leftist they are not homogenously so. As individuals all those who work in the relevant jobs are active in their trade unions. Some are also active in political parties. As a group, however, the community has no commitment to any political party. The community certainly values this independence and so do some of its friends. A political study group is held weekly in the community. This is attended by local workers and students who find there a freer and less sectarian atmosphere than in political parties or groups. This study group was originally started on the initiative of former students of the evening school whose political consciousness had been raised by attending the course.

Many in the commune vote communist. They regard the programme of the Italian Communist party as the right programme for change for Italy now, and the Marxist analysis of history – that history develops out of the clash of economic interests and specifically the struggle of classes – as useful. But when Marx and his followers become 'metaphysical' and by the proofs of dialectical materialism claim certainty for their view of history, the Protestants draw back. They put 'their trust in the kingdom' and the kingdom is not the same as the Marxist view of history. Because it happens to be the case that the dream of the Marxist metaphysicians is, as a community member said, 'a secular version of the kingdom' the believers and non-believers in Cinisello can work together with and on behalf of the working class. But no Protestant in Cinisello would say that the kingdom is to be found on earth.

The Cinisello community has been together since 1968. The members attribute their success to the evening school. Without it they would have become introspective. With it the dynamic of the original vision has been maintained and new members introduced. It may be that the community has prospered just because it has been prepared to develop and change, though so far always within the lines of the original vision.

The vision and work of Cinisello is best understood within the context of Italian Protestantism and primarily within the context of the thinking of FGEI. Cinisello is not only in some ways self-consciously Protestant, but also identified as part of the Italian Protestant institutional church. This in itself is significant. It is not, as many other communities are, on the fringe of a church, but the pace-setter of a church which is itself on the fringe of Italian society.

6

Student Christian Movement
Community House
Birmingham

During 1973 the Student Christian Movement of Great Britain and Ireland decided to sink some of its funds in residential property across its territory. Houses were bought in university towns with active SCM branches and were made available for student accommodation. It was intended that these should be communal experiments; some would be supported by resident members of SCM staff.

Why, it will surely be asked, did an organization of student groups make a decision of this sort?

During the sixties and early seventies the SCM was the unofficial Christian representative at the table of educational upheaval. In this role it was open to some of the ideas and close to some of the experiments which have arisen out of the ferment in the universities of Western Europe. In chapter 1 it was suggested that the current interest in communal living arose, at least in part, out of this ferment. Informal experiments were starting in many places; the SCM was eager to encourage Christian communes. Various members had already been instrumental in the establishment of the Blackheath Commune in London and the Newhaven Commune in Edinburgh.[1]

The decision was therefore taken to put some of the Movement's inherited wealth into property to enable students and others to participate in communal experiments. In a small way the SCM would also be helping the student accommodation problem, at that time acute.

As a result of this decision houses were bought in the university centres of Cardiff, Dublin, Birmingham and Bristol. In addition groups of students in Oxford and St Andrews, who had each made a decision to live together, persuaded the SCM administration to sponsor them. These latter two experiments, which sprang from the aspiration of particular groups of students, soon accomplished their aims of being both residential communities and also centres of student activity.

As a further development of all this interest in communal living the SCM headquarters were moved out of London in 1974 to Wick Court, a Jacobean mansion near Bristol, where the central staff attempted to live communally.

The four houses first mentioned, the initiative for which had come from the organization, met with considerable problems. This chapter describes the Community House in Birmingham.

The description is mainly in the words of two of the members of the community, beginning with a 'statement of intent' and continuing with excerpts of three tape-recorded conversations which the author had with these members. This chapter is, unlike the preceding four which are more in the way of cameos capturing the communities at a particular period in time, more of an historical exercise. It covers the first year in the community's life.

During the spring of 1973 funds were made available for the purchase of a house and that summer suitable accommodation was found. Soon afterwards two SCM secretaries appointed to work among the students in England, and who had been deputed to establish the House (we shall call them Eva and John), drew up this statement of intent.

We have purchased two medium-sized houses in Birmingham which we are opening as an SCM community house. The houses are situated in Springfield, a fairly conventional residential area three miles away from the city centre.

Each house has six rooms, plus plenty of cooking, bathroom and toilet facilities. The community house will operate as a single unit with the following facilities: SCM English regional office; residential accommodation for the two secretaries – plus others who want to join them to live on a long-term communal basis; overnight/short-stay accommodation for SCM members and friends; catering and sleeping facilities for week-end conferences for up to twenty-five people. The house will also provide office accommodation for Third World Publications,[2] and their full-time worker will live with the residential community.

It is Eva and John's intention that the Community house should provide the opportunity for developing new and interesting ways of servicing and enriching the local branch of SCM groups everywhere, but obviously they already have some idea of how they would like the Community House to operate on a day-to-day basis. For example, the permanent residents will live communally, hopefully as an experimenting Christian community, serving as an example to others searching for more liberating alternatives to the constraining and oppressive influences of society. Anyone will be welcome to become part of this community for a long-term

or a short-term period. The house will also have a sustaining and supportive role for fringe Christians who may simply want a place to
'talk things through' or 'sort themselves out' or just to meet like-
minded people to have discussions – hence the availability of overnight/
short-stay accommodation.

In a way we are saying: 'Let's make a start, somewhere, at *living* this
Christian revolution thing.' This is a tremendous risk for the Movement
to take, particularly when the bulk of the students we come into contact
with are living in situations pretty remote from any revolution. Eva and
John are determined that by their work on campuses and by their welcoming students to stay at the Community House, they will be able to
bridge the gap between the theory and practice of developing alternative
life-styles.[3]

In November 1973, when the House had been open two months, I
made my first visit. John and Eva had found four others to make up
their numbers, including one unsupported mother who had brought
her baby with her. The fact that they had had to find these others had
shown them something.

Eva: The natural process of a group of people who get on together
and have some kind of fellowship, finding a place to live together,
has been about-turned. We were given a job-brief, told to start a
community house and arrived in a town totally fresh. The people
who move in, move in totally green. We don't know them; they
don't know us, really. There's also a certain amount of pressure to
get the thing off the ground quickly. Whether we have made the
right choice about the membership of the house we don't know.

Told to start a community house . . . but what made them willing to
identify with this experiment? Why did they want to live communally?

Eva: Communal living is for me personally the only answer in the
really long run. I find it relatively easy to relate to people spontane-
ously. I really enjoy meeting lots of people and developing relationships and I have a bit of a problem when the relationship
becomes totally exclusive. Living communally, particularly in an
urban house, is a fantastic way of living, because there are always
people around and it's always bubbling and thriving. One can get
to know people to a considerable depth provided one's open and
honest and warm and human enough about it.

John: It was part of a development of my own personal beliefs and
feelings. I find the nuclear family a bit frustrating and stultifying
and I was looking for an alternative setting for the basis of relating to other people. There was also the consideration that radical

Christians outside the church need some kind of community. I certainly feel the need for a community which will have a supportive and sustaining role, might engage in some kind of worship and celebration, and will simply be a place where ideas can be worked out and thrashed out.

But what makes a community? Eva's answer dealt with the importance of fellowship, rather than shared physical arrangements.

Eva: It's obviously not just a group of young people living together with separate rooms, sharing a living-room and pooling a kitty. There has to be some kind of fellowship and spiritual bond between the people. Whatever it is it doesn't have to be Christian, but there has to be some reason for wanting to be together and involved in this house other than just being jolly good friends or just having a boarding-house. I feel strongly that that is lacking in so many places where people are living. It's just not enough to throw people together and have polite conversation. What we'd like to see is people sharing their evenings together; we're anti having a television, that might interrupt this process. We're hoping eventually that they'll celebrate together. This obviously won't be a traditional Christian celebration, but something spontaneous, that happens out of the community to celebrate our mutual joys, fears and anguishes, us as a group.

So, were they looking for anything special in those who joined them?

Eva: Yes, I'd like to find some kind of spiritual commitment in the people here. I'd not like to exclude anybody who uses texts other than the Bible as a background. I've met an awful lot of people who obviously have this tangible spirituality about them who are not Christian. This spirituality makes people human.

John differed here.

John: Their motivation and reason for doing things should in some way be connected with belief in the Christian gospels and what the life of Christ represented, and the examination of what that means. Otherwise I just feel you've got nothing in common. That may sound a bit shivery, but I think we're just saying that we want to know that somewhere along the line that person keeps ticking because of some desire to work out what the Christian thing is all about.

But, in fact, of the other members of the community at that stage, only one shared both their ideals about communal living and their Christian commitment. Indeed it was probably true that John and Eva felt that they had more in common with certain others outside the house.

John: Some evenings when we have people round here, who might not be people in the community, but other political people or people connected with different Christian groups, we'll have a really good talk and feel really close, but you won't be able to put your finger on anything, and you think, especially afterwards, 'something was there'.

A community established by a committee will of necessity run up against problems which do not afflict communities resulting from the matured convictions of their members. The very fact that being in the house was part of John and Eva's jobs meant that the House would only be home as long as they remained in the job. How did they feel about this?

John: It is very difficult to get any notion of permanence about the place when you know that there's a possibility you'll only be here for two years. The whole concept of permanence within life, within relationships, is something which I'm questioning pretty fundamentally.[4]

Eva: We're creating something with a time-limit to it, certainly as far as we are concerned. We are always keeping an ear open for the type of project we'd like to be involved in for ever, with no time-limit to it; for myself a rural commune, with urban links, a particular project of its own and one which obviously has a spiritual fellowship to it.

These were their feelings in November 1973. By March 1974 when I lived with them again the community had settled down into a routine. The numbers had grown to seven adults and two children. Few of the more daring visions of the statement of intent (quoted at the beginning of this chapter) had become reality. But, in terms of the physical arrangements of the House, much had been achieved.

Eva: We eat our evening meal together, taking it in turns to cook it. Everybody puts £3 per week into the kitty for housekeeping and £2.50 a month for electricity and gas.
We've just purchased a washing machine towards which every-

body paid £1. It was bought in an auction sale for £7, but it works. We've also communally purchased tools and a vacuum cleaner.

As far as equipment which people have got themselves is concerned, except in a few exceptional cases these are offered to communal use, like the toaster, the hi-fi set and the sewing machine. We share what we've got and generally put in the same amount for things that we haven't got and which have to be purchased. We thought at great length of dividing up according to salaries and having a proportion of each salary put into the kitty. But only one of us earns much more than everyone else in the house because he's on a teacher's salary. It really wouldn't make all that difference between the rest of us – one who is on Social Security, John and me who are on SCM salaries, the Third World Publications secretary on a similar salary and another who is an auxiliary nurse. We do share two of the three ancient cars we have between us. The keys are always in the car or hanging on the board in the office or in the kitchen, and you just take one if you want to and put some petrol in it.

Physical arrangements such as these provide the framework of any community; without them there is little in common. If a group of people cannot co-operate with each other to the extent of sharing certain possessions and domestic jobs, little progress can be made toward realizing the grander visions. In the case of this House, however, once the physical arrangements had been agreed on, the group faltered.

Eva: One of us is hot on the notion that a community needs a project and can't feed on itself. Another would argue that a community must be at peace with itself before it can venture forth. The first would say that's wasting time and you've got to have a project and the project will bring you together. This debate has been going on since November.

We've had sessions together and you can divide these in two. Some are business sessions, which happen over extended meals. We just work out the hassles of the bills which have come in, talk about what we're going to plant in the garden and things like: the loo's blocked, who can unblock it? We have also had 'honesty-sessions'. In one of these we talked about how we felt about each other and about our vision of the community, the kingdom and so on. This 'honesty-session' happened because I called it, and I called it because there were a whole lot of things which hadn't been talked

through. One member was fairly unhappy and obviously unhappy. We hadn't been alone for a long time, so I thought we
might as well have an 'honesty-session'.

Bearing in mind that only three of the seven adult members had
actually had ideals about communal living from the start it was an
achievement that everybody was prepared to talk about this. But it
would not be true to say that the problems arising from the way the
House had been founded were being entirely overcome. John and
Eva felt that there was not enough in common between the members
of the community for them to be able to express themselves in worship and celebration.[5] The worship issue was a symbol of the differing
ideas of those three in the community on the one hand who had
definite opinions about communal living and Christian commitment
and everybody else on the other.

But the intention of the committee which had decided upon the
Birmingham Community House had been that John and Eva should
find local students with similiar ideas to themselves to fill it. What
had gone wrong?

Eva: We bumped up immediately against the fact that there were no
   students to fill the place. We offered it to Christian students we
   knew at Aston University, where there is a branch of SCM, and at
   Birmingham University. Nobody bit. I think we probably played
   the vision line a little too hard. A lot of students felt they wanted
   to be students first and not let 'alternative projects' interfere with
   their examinations and things.

So, because 'no students bit' (at that stage) others had to be
attracted. There was no shortage of others.

Eva: Aspiring members of the House were presented with a statement
   of our aims for the House, laying heavy emphasis on its SCM
   orientation and the Christian bias and we presumed this would be
   interpreted constructively. But . . . you can't find out if they really
   understand what the issues are until you live with them and they
   start expressing themselves and doing things.

Quite apart from their own eagerness to find suitable others for
the House, John and Eva faced early on the moral dilemma which
confronts every community: 'How open shall we be? Can we ever
turn away the needy when they come (literally) to our door?' Eva
described their first experience of this dilemma.

Eva: Carol was a homeless, unsupported mother and pregnant again. Her brother, a theological student in Birmingham who was round at the House a great deal, suggested that she be allowed a room in the House. We said 'Yes', and she arrived. The first time John sat down to talk to her and automatically assumed she had some sort of vision as well she burst out crying and said 'I'm just an ordinary housewife – I just need somewhere for myself and my baby.' John and I were so overwhelmed by this sudden outburst that we said, 'Calm down; be welcome here', and left it at that. But then recently we had an absolutely super family staying here who had a vision; they were professedly Christian as well. Their kids were just totally natural and adaptable. They were really super to have around. They participated in the evening meal and brought the level of discussion up. It would have been nice if there had been room for them to stay on. But there was no room. What does one do? Can one throw people out? Does that family, having a vision, override our being human to people?

Although John and Eva had to face this moral dilemma from early on, they were able to bring into contact with the House others with whom they really wanted to share their vision. This meant in the first place Third World Publications, a small non-profit-making business which imports books and pamphlets from the Third World.

Eva: I feel that one of the major assets of having Third World Publications on the premises is that it gives you something to come to other than just an SCM community house. We were also hoping that a group who were into organic farming and wanted to use our back garden to experiment with different kinds of compost would materialize. And then there's a printing-press in the shed, which is another focus in its own right. This is available to anyone who wants to use it.

And at Christmas the House was used for an Open Christmas for the homeless; meals were cooked there and other preparations made. In addition the House was subject to a continuous stream of visitors which swelled to a torrent when conferences organized by the SCM took place in or around it.

Eva: But the house is a shell with interesting things going on within it; there's nobody who's staked their lives. Not even us. I know this isn't my final abode, and I'm not really ploughing myself into it totally. It's a total thing for two years but I know it will come to an end. It will come to an end for everyone else too.

Soon after this previous conversation John and Eva decided to leave the House within a few months, not wishing (as John put it) to live any longer with the 'fruits of our own mistakes'. During the summer John moved to another job within the SCM and joined the resident community at the SCM headquarters. Eva and some friends began a rural community in East Anglia. Both hoped that in these situations they would find it easier to realize their frustrated ideals.

Some months later I talked to John about the first year of the House's existence. He analysed the mistakes that had been made. In the first place:

John: A community is a group which is committed to each other first before it lives together. That wasn't true in our case. It could have been true if Eva and I had been prepared to live in two empty houses for six months and waited to see what emerged from contacts which we made. We felt a little bit paranoid about living in empty houses and a little bit paranoid about being in a city in which neither of us had any contacts. You find it very easy to get into a situation in which, if you're not strong, you feel obliged to let someone come in. There was only one person whom we consciously solicited into joining us.

A particular problem linked with this was that of the differing attitudes to communal living, even in quite trivial contexts.

John: I would have been a lot happier with structures and rotas, while Eva from the beginning said she wanted these to emerge naturally. It was well into November before we had the first meeting when we spoke about cleaning the house. She said nobody should feel obliged to cook because it's their night. Similarly you only clean up when the place is messy. That doesn't take account of people's different levels of tolerance of dirt.

And more fundamentally:

John: Also two people gave the impression eventually of wanting the good things from a community, like not living on their own, without wanting to generate any kind of commitment to the people they lived with. Consequently they took the advantages of the communal situation, and yet were not able to give anything themselves . . .

It's a rule in a number of monastic communities that if there are things with which you disagree which involve a third party you don't talk about them without that third party being there. From the very beginning Eva and I would shut ourselves in our office and have long raps about what was wrong with the House, and this would involve talking about the other people in the House. Other people would get the impression that we were ganging up.

John here put his finger on an important point. It appeared that there were two camps in the House. While he and Eva were in positions of leadership in the community, others were not eager to take responsibility. After they left, however, there was an interval before the next SCM staff member arrived and the management of the House, its activities and its finances were handed over to the inhabitants as a group. 'This immediately' (I quote from a letter I received from Eva at the end of 1974) 'increased the commitment and concern of all the residents for the place, and they rapidly began to feel it was their place, they spent much time in the garden, organized themselves as a centre where battered wives could find crash accommodation, and are actually running the Open Christmas in Birmingham from the House.'

In starting the Birmingham Community House there was a positive achievement to record. There were six or seven people living together for a long time instead of living on their own. They shared a great deal. That this sharing rarely extended beyond the practicalities of day-to-day living is something emphasized by the disillusioned explanations of the preceding paragraphs. But only those who had begun with such high expectations had experienced this disillusionment. One member, who had not been fired with a vision when she moved into the House said that she had changed in her six months there, and would certainly live communally again. To an outsider too the House had a homeliness and offered a mutual support of which some of the inhabitants were perhaps not aware.

But this community was different in many ways from the other four described in this book. To begin with it was established directly by an organization while all the others had founded themselves, so to speak. The support of a parent institution did bring a few advantages, such as financial security. But the relationship of the House to the parent body was never properly defined; nobody was sure, for example, how far the House was answerable to the SCM. Also the other community members behaved as if the SCM's representatives,

John and Eva, were responsible for the House and for the most part did not participate in its running until they left.

A second difference from the other communities was that John and Eva were set down in a place and (as they put it) expected to create an instant commune. In all the other four communities described here it was more or less the case that a group of people who already knew each other and had a common purpose, had become convinced that they would profit from living together communally. Having started to put their conviction into practice they attracted others who were impressed by their venture and joined them. This was more or less the pattern. John and Eva, on the other hand, started with just themselves and for reasons already mentioned, were keen to fill the House as quickly as possible. Though arrangements for shared day-to-day living were successfully worked out these did not spring from the slowly-matured convictions of the group and were rather like the seed that fell on rocky ground in the parable and which sprang up quickly, but then could grow no more because the soil was shallow.

And thirdly, there was no defined communal aim or activity. Of course the community had certain common interests and performed certain common activities. But if one thinks of the other four groups described in this book one realizes that these all have shared aims and activities to which all members are committed. Indeed that is part of the commitment which the members of those groups have made to one another. At Emmaus it is a simple life-style and the rag-and-bone business, at Laurentiuskonvent it is peace and peace-work, at Greenbus it is living off the land and openness to penniless wanderers, and at Cinisello it is political change in Italy and the evening-school. It was in the nature of the Community House that it had no comparable shared aim or activity.

These seem the most striking differences from the other communities. The Community House was an experiment of a particular kind and within limited terms was not unsuccessful. In both its style and its frustrations it is not untypical of many informal communities which come and go every year in Western Europe.

7

Christian Radicalism

> We do not see the vital point
> That 'tis the eighth, most deadly, sin
> To wail, 'The world is out of joint'—
> And not attempt to put it in.[1]

These pungent lines of Charles Sorley are over seventy years old. It is still the case that there are more who wail that the world is out of joint than attempt to put it in. Yet one of the most striking impressions one gains of these five communities is that they are all attempting (with varying degrees of success, certainly, but still attempting) to put the world in joint. Though they make their wail, they do not stop at it.

This chapter and the next will look at this combination of criticism and reconstruction; this chapter discussing the sources of the groups' thinking. Where do they get their ideas and inspiration from?

There are apparently two main sources, the Christian tradition (in the broadest sense of the term) and contemporary radical thought. What, first, is meant by the 'Christian tradition'?

Obviously one begins with the Bible, primary in every sense to the Christian tradition. The New Testament and what it says of Jesus is the first point of reference. However we would not find in the five communities chapter and verse justification of their activities and way of life.

Then there is all the thinking, teaching and action which have made up two thousand years of Christianity. Each country and sometimes each locality differs here and the communities tended to reflect the emphases of their particular traditions. At Laurentiuskonvent, for example, the community considered itself part of the German

Protestant Church and was greatly influenced by the example of the Confessing Church. At Cinisello a history of oppression as a religious minority brings the Italian Protestants nearer to the contemporary oppressed working class than to Catholics who are their fellow Christians. At Glastonbury it was clear that Greenbus had grown up amidst the riches of local legend. It was Emmaus who most frequently shared a eucharist; its founders were Roman Catholic.

In all five cases it was the position of the founder or founding members which was crucial. The greater the closeness of the leading members of the group to a particular confessional tradition, for example, the more that group was influenced by that tradition's practice and theological perspective. At SCM Birmingham, where the leading members were not close to their confessional traditions, there was no visible influence from any particular denomination.

But the richness of the past Christian tradition for the five groups is supplemented by contemporary influences. No Christian receives the inspiration and example of Christ outside the world to which he belongs. Taking only the most obvious example, the gospel tells us that we must love one another and in Christ's actions and parables gives us paradigms, but we can only act out the command of love as the contemporary situation requires.

What is understood to be required will obviously vary from person to person. And in the present context each of the five communities saw something different as required of them. But there were also common factors – namely a radical critique of society and a revolutionary vision.

The five communities were, by and large, critical of rather than sympathetic to contemporary society. And so the Christian tradition is supplemented by a second main source of influence, that body of ideas which is here called 'contemporary radical thought', for want of a better term.

What is meant by this phrase? Only examples which will follow can make its use clearer. By 'radical thought' is meant here that modern spectrum of ideas which pose a challenge to the very roots (as the word 'radical' implies) of our social assumptions, values, behaviour and structures. Because it is a challenge which strikes at the roots, no social edifice (in the broadest sense of the word) can remain unscathed, neither political and economic structures and policies, nor manifestations of religion, nor sexual attitudes and behaviour, nor social conventions of any kind.

Radical thought both analyses how and why the world is out of joint and also tries to find alternatives, in ways of putting it back. More, as Sorley complained, are interested in analysis than in reconstruction. For though a radical analysis of society, like the gospel, demands a response, not everybody both hears the word and does it. These five communities, however, tend to be made up of those who have become aware of serious shortcomings in the social fabric, discussed the issues and felt that a response was demanded of them. At some point they decided to live communally. This may only have been when a particular opening presented itself. They were conscious that in joining any one of these five communities they were implicitly taking up a critical stance in relation to society.

These two sources of influence, the Christian tradition and contemporary radical thought, are not of course really neat packages nor is an individual likely to separate them out as has been done here. For most of the community members the marriage of these two was an entirely obvious match.

But this is a match which by no means everybody would regard as obvious, or even desirable. It would be difficult to claim that all, even most, Christians in the Western world see even a remote connection between the gospel and a radical critique of society. The situation is different in Africa, Latin America and some parts of Asia, as well as in the Eastern bloc, where the gospel inspires much of the criticism of 'the powers that be'.[2] And, moreover, this connection is one which has been made by certain groups in Western Europe throughout the Christian era, in times and places in which Christianity has had many different statuses.

These groups include some of the communities which foreran our own intentional communities. The earliest monastic communities of Egypt were doing more than escaping from anti-Christian Roman emperors. They were deeply critical of Roman civilization. This element reappeared in the monastic innovators of later centuries, especially St Bernard (founder of the Cistercians), St Francis and St Bruno (founder of the Carthusians). All these men offered a Christian critique of their age. And among those intentional communities which did not come to be labelled monastic, many groups, from the Diggers of the mid-seventeenth century to the present-day communities mentioned in chapter 1 have tried to apply the teaching of the gospel in an analysis of the social order.

So how in these five communities of the present day have Christianity and radical thought together been their inspiration?

(i) The Choice to Live Communally

The first answer is in their very choice to live communally. As was said in chapter 1, Christian communities are as old as Christians; secular communities on the other hand have only existed since the middle of the last century but have greatly increased in number since the mid-sixties. The increase in communal groups in general has brought with it a corresponding growth in the number of Christian communities.

The choice of these five groups to live communally was made against the background of a rich Christian tradition of communal living and (except in the case of Laurentiuskonvent) the recent growth of communities of all sorts as a response to the contemporary world.

The Christian tradition of communal living begins in the New Testament. Nobody in any of the communities actually leapt for their Bible and turned up the biblical accounts of communitarianism, Acts 2.42–47 and 4.32–35. But all were aware of the many dimensions of communal life within New Testament Christianity; common goods, common worship, common life, common witness, common tasks. Any emphasis they made tended to stem from their confessional background rather than from these biblical accounts. The extent of their debt to the monastic tradition for example varied accordingly. Perhaps when a Briton thinks of examples of Christian communities he thinks immediately of the monastic orders, but it must be remembered that monastic life is foreign to most of the Protestant churches of Western Europe. In Italy Cinisello had no monastic communities within its tradition. Their models went no further back apparently than the Confessing Church in Germany and recent Protestant experiments like the Agape and Riesi communities in Italy. In West Germany Laurentiuskonvent looked more to the communities of nineteenth-century Anglicanism, notably the Society of the Sacred Mission and the Community of the Resurrection.[3] At Emmaus, on the other hand, with two Franciscans within the community there was a conscious link with the mendicant orders. The two English communities also, as one might expect in a country in which there are both Anglican and Roman Catholic religious orders, were both familiar with monastic models. Greenbus lived consciously according to a monastic rhythm of life and its leader wanted to live more specifically by the example of St Bernard, founder of the Cistercian order. The Birmingham Community House was aware of specific practices in monastic communities but did not in general have any conscious monastic model.

The monastic tradition is not solely in the past. New religious orders are still being born and one in particular has exerted an enormous influence on other contemporary Christian communities. This is the ecumenical Taizé Community[4] in France, now over thirty years old. This community has become a focus in the search of many people, especially those who are young, for an authentic Christian faith which combines the elements of 'struggle and contemplation'. The Taizé Community has its own life of work, prayer and meals which goes on in spite of the invading visitors who in the early seventies totalled on average a hundred thousand a year.

'Struggle and contemplation' – the struggle for a more human world and the contemplation which through prayer will give strength for the struggle – are the key words.

Of the five groups only Cinisello did not admit to having gained inspiration from contact with the Taizé Community. Each of the other four gained a different inspiration from Taizé. Greenbus and Laurentiuskonvent found the discipline of Taizé an inspiration for their own. One of the Laurentiuskonvent brothers had indeed been a novice at Taizé. Greenbus had, like Taizé, a thrice-daily office and repeated each day words which had come out of the 1970 gatherings there.[5] The leader of Greenbus had spent a great deal of time with the Taizé brothers. In 1972 the Emmaus community took a break and went to Taizé as a group. They came back with a chalice and patten (Laurentiuskonvent also possessed a set made by the Taizé brothers) and a strengthened resolve. A number of present and past members of the Emmaus group had been directed to it by brothers at Taizé who thought highly of it. Two members of the SCM Birmingham house went to Taizé at Easter 1974, and though they had mixed feelings about the youthful invasion, they were deeply impressed by the community itself.

Taizé is a specific model from the Christian tradition. As has already been said, 'secular' communes grew out of the upsurge in radical thought at the end of the sixties.[6] These generally lacked the formality and discipline which characterizes monastic communities. Four of our five communities (Laurentiuskonvent being the exception) are also considerably less formal and in some cases considerably less disciplined than their monastic forbears. This whole issue will be discussed in chapter 9.

The five communities have absorbed from contemporary radical thought the idea that to live communally is in itself an act of dissent. Earlier in this chapter it was suggested that communal groups in earlier times often applied the teaching of the gospels in an analysis of the social order. Some contemporary groups go one stage further and see the actual state of living communally as an act of witness to their dissent. Communal living as an act of dissent is in part the subject of the next chapter.

(ii) Visions

A second way in which the Christian tradition and contemporary radical thought come together in these five communities is in their visions. All intentional communities are born out of a vision or perhaps many visions. There may indeed be as many visions as members; there are certainly as many visions as communities.

In the Christian tradition visions have often been expressed in the language of beliefs about the kingdom of God. This is no less true of the five communities. Their visions of the future relate to their own communities in particular, where they are attempting to live out their faith. But through the creation of their own communities all five are aiming for the renewal of the world, and as one theologian has expressed it, 'the renewal of the world on the lines of God's original purpose'.[7]

There is a tension here, between the future and the present. The vision is for the future, but it must to some extent be realized in the present. The five communities believe that a start must be made somewhere on changing the world as they think Christ would change it. And wherever that start is made it embodies the beginning of the kingdom. But because the kingdom is always in the future the embodiment of it is always a process of growth and never static. They are in fact anticipating the kingdom in what they do and hoping for it in their strivings.

The present importance of the kingdom is in one sense a result of widespread dissatisfaction with contemporary society. Another contemporary theologian, Jürgen Moltmann, has linked the Christian future hope with a process of transforming the world. He writes of 'a transformation of the world in expectation of a divine transformation'.[8]

The theology of the kingdom can make sense of, or at least co-exist with, visions of radical thought which bear no obvious connection to Christianity. Two particular strands of visionary thought which are part of contemporary radical thought appear in the thinking of two of the five communities. At Cinisello Marxist eschatology, the necessary victory of the working class which will result from the dialectical process of history, commands a considerable following. And at Glastonbury Greenbus included a number of people whose Christian vision was bound up with local Arthurian legend. The second coming of Arthur is difficult to distinguish from the second coming of Christ; now it represents the hoped for triumph of Glastonbury visions of a balanced, sensitive, artistic and spiritually developed world. In both Cinisello and Glastonbury the visions which the contemporary world has thrown up mingle and co-exist with visions which are more readily recognized as Christian.

(iii) Tasks

The nature of the visions is clear from the tasks which the communities undertake and this is the third area in which Christianity and contemporary radical thought have come together. Each community acts out New Testament teaching in the way which seems most appropriate. And what seems most appropriate depends largely on the areas needful of action identified by radical thought. The tasks of Emmaus and Greenbus emphasize material poverty. Christ himself exemplified this, but in today's world material poverty is bound up with ecology. Emmaus has chosen to sell others' throw-outs, Greenbus to grow its own food. In another century these tasks might be totally inappropriate. Cinisello and Laurentiuskonvent, on the other hand, emphasize political action. Both understand that this is enjoined upon the Christian community by Christ's commandment of love, since they believe that 'love', though it includes individual acts of charity, entails more than these. In today's world Cinisello interprets its task as educational, Laurentiuskonvent engages in peace work. Again these tasks of political action might in another century be totally inappropriate.

The tasks of both Emmaus and Greenbus are concerned with what they take to be the ecological dislocation of Western society. Emmaus protests against extravagant consumption by gathering and selling throw-outs and sending the proceeds to those who have nothing to consume. Greenbus has a different emphasis, though sharing the criticisms which are implied in Emmaus' activities. Greenbus' protest against ecological dislocation is in moving towards supporting itself from the land. The basic premise of these standpoints is that the relationship of man to nature is not entirely separate from the relationship of man with man. These communities, while emphasizing the harmonious co-operation which should exist between man and nature, also believe that their doors should be open to fellow-men who need them, thus making explicit their desire for a similar relationship between man and man.

Emmaus and Greenbus in attacking ecological dislocation and practising material poverty have not chosen to do so uninfluenced. While it would be difficult to identify the chain of influences which have acted upon them it is easier to point to others who have articulated similar concerns. These others include many rural communes, who are critical of the relationships between man and man, and man and nature. Such criticism extends beyond these particular points. In the words of the Commune Movement:

> (People) have lost the art of providing themselves with the basic necessities of life, or if they have not lost the art they have certainly lost the opportunity, for they have been dispossessed of the Earth and have been herded into the factories and offices . . . Who among herded humanity is fortunate enough to discover adventure and what mind is still free enough to see inspiration among the mass of mediocrity and subjugation of individuality? . . . The natural environment has been destroyed and in its place we have a panorama of brick and tarmac, interspersed with dreary parks and gardens that look more and more like plastic . . . In a welfare society we see the rejections of the sick, the old and the lonely; we have no real answer to the care of old age.[9]

The main tasks of Laurentiuskonvent and Cinisello, on the other hand, though equally influenced by radical thought, are very different from those of Emmaus and Greenbus. The pithy distinction between them might be that while the latter are ascetic, the former are activist. Laurentiuskonvent and Cinisello share with each other (and with individuals in the Birmingham Community House) a deeply-felt criticism of social structures. There the similarity ends, for while Cinisello's sphere of action is educational deprivation, Laurentiuskonvent is concerned above all to counter the violence which the social structures do to personal, social and international relationships. This community enables broken individuals to be restored at the Malteserhof. It works to eradicate the violence of social disorientation. It brings about volunteer service in the hope that individuals can contribute to the healing of the sores which fester in the relationships between Europe and the Third World. Cinisello, on the other hand, while its work is less individual-centred than that of the Laurentiuskonvent, lays the same emphasis on the analysis of social structures and the mutual effect that the individual and society can have upon each other. Cinisello's way into the problems caused by the clash of interest between society and the individual is the nurture of local, educationally deprived teenagers. The community hopes that their pupils as individuals and as a group will become aware of their situation in the locality and how they can change it. The specific tasks of Laurentiuskonvent and Cinisello owe much to contemporary discussions about the meaning of violence and about educational content and method.

In summary, these five communities are fired by both the Christian tradition and contemporary radical thought. Communal living has become an accepted response for many of those who are critical of our contemporary society, but it is a response deeply rooted in the Christian tradition. The tasks which the communities undertake are an attempt to make concrete their visions. Broadly speaking, the gospel tells them what principles to live by, and contemporary social criticism lights up the issues on which to concentrate.

8

A New Exodus

(i) Compartments

'If the God who called them to life,' wrote Jürgen Moltmann, 'should expect of them something other than what modern industrial society expects and requires of them, then Christians must venture an exodus and regard their social roles as a new Babylonian exile.'[1]

In the last chapter it was argued that these five communities are more critical of than sympathetic to contemporary society, and that this criticism gives expression to their Christian faith. But, as the contemporary German theologian, Jürgen Moltmann, suggests in the passage just quoted, our society does not expect this of Christianity. Our society does not expect Christians to take up critical positions. What in fact it does expect and how these five communities frustrate those expectations is the subject of this chapter.

What then are the roles, or perhaps better the functions, of Christianity in Western industrial society? Or, to put it another way, where is it that our society invokes Christianity in order to give itself meaning?

It invokes it firstly in certain religious ceremonies. Peter Berger identifies the institutions of the state and the family as those areas of life in which the symbolism of religious ceremonial is most intensively employed.

> Even at a point of far-reaching secularization of everyday life as lived at work and in the relationships that surround work one may still find religious symbols attached to the institutions of state and family. For instance, at a point where everyone takes for granted that 'religion stops at the factory gate' it may nevertheless be also taken for granted that one does not inaugurate either a war or a marriage without the traditional religious symbolizations.[2]

In Britain, for example, not only wars, but also coronations, the daily business of Parliament and certain civic occasions are accompanied by religious ceremonies. Christianity here plays the role of the '*cultus publicus*', the official religion, a role which it inherited from the Roman state religion.[3] As in ancient Rome the God or gods of the 'official religion' have to be placated before any important enterprise is begun. This role does not imply that the State is itself a religious institution or even that religious teachings are applied in the affairs of the State.

The life of the family, too, is inextricably bound up with Christian ceremonial. At the time of writing a majority of Britons accompany their progress from the cradle to the grave with Christian ceremonies – baptism, marriage and funeral services – in church. All these ceremonies are rituals which have significance for the family as well as for the individual within the family. They mark respectively entry to the family, the creation of a new family and exit from the family with the promise however of reunion in an afterlife. Partly because these Christian ceremonies are so clearly related to the critical points in the life of a family, but also because of other factors, such as Christ's birth into an earthly family, Christianity is seen to give meaning to the family institution. This point will be discussed later in connection with the contrast between community and family.

But when someone describes Western Europe as Christian, he is probably thinking not so much of ceremonies as of the other chief social function of Christianity. This is the moral guidance which Christianity gives about sexual behaviour, truthfulness, behaviour to one's neighbour and so on. But Christian moral teaching is not thought to go further than this. It is, for example, assumed that Christianity has nothing to say about ethics at the work-place or about the financial and political decisions and policies of individuals and institutions. In these areas of activity decisions are made in the light of aims and standards of behaviour which are not consciously Christian. (More will be said about this later.) Instead Christianity is expected to content itself with guiding moral behaviour in a limited part of life, namely what we do as families, how we conduct our personal relationships and spare-time activities. The second social function of Christianity is thus to be found in the 'private sphere' of our lives.

These are the general social functions expected and required of Christianity by modern industrial society – very different from the picture we get from the communities. If we look back a few centuries the picture is also different. The social functions of the Christian religion were far from restricted. For good or for ill our medieval ancestors in Western Europe used the language and concepts of Christianity to understand everything in their world. The Christianity which they knew was not a 'religion' in the way that we understand the word but a system of revealed truth which explained the world as it was by reference to God's acts of creation, the Fall and inherent sinfulness of man, God's saving act in Christ on the cross and his promise of resurrection after death. This system constituted more than an 'approved' belief-system; it made sense of the everyday experiences of medieval man and was accepted as the way of interpreting that experience.

Pluralism – competing systems of interpreting the world – was unknown. Christianity was without serious competitors. The church had occasionally competitors who claimed alternative interpretations of revealed truth, but almost nobody thought to challenge Christianity itself. There were two inseparable correlatives of this unchallenged belief-system, which ensured that it underrode every sphere of life. First, theology was the basis of ethics, economics, politics, commerce and all other areas of thought which we now consider separate. Secondly, Christianity was understood to provide the moral foundation of all behaviour in every sphere of life, whether that morality was actually practised or not. In the case of economics for instance, the situation when the Age of the Reformation begins is that

> economics is still a branch of ethics, and ethics of theology; all human activities are treated as falling within a single scheme, whose character is determined by the spiritual destiny of mankind; the appeal of theorists is to natural law, not to utility; the legitimacy of economic transactions is tried by reference, less to the movements of the market, than to moral standards derived from the traditional teaching of the Christian Church.[4]

During the Reformation period the process of the emancipation of 'social doctrine' from theology began. The disciplines of thought about man in society, political theory, economics, commerce, were then emerging. Later sociology was added to these. In medieval Western Europe these too had been simply part of theology and subject to the laws and moral teaching of Christianity. They had had no separate identity or realm of their own. Gradually they came to acquire their own spheres of relevance and their own internally consistent rules. In the words of R. H. Tawney:

The theological mould which shaped political theory from the Middle Ages to the seventeenth century is broken; politics becomes a science, ultimately a group of sciences, and theology at best one science among others. Reason takes the place of revelation, and the criterion of political institutions is expediency, not religious authority. Religion, ceasing to be the master-interest of mankind, dwindles into a department of life with boundaries which it is extravagant to overstep.[5]

The consequence of the emancipation of spheres like politics, economics and commerce from the hold of theology was the necessarily decreasing application of Christian values in these areas of life. It could not be otherwise. With theological concepts thought to be irrelevant to an ever-increasing number of spheres of life moral decisions came to be made outside the framework of Christian values. Indeed each sphere of human activity developed its own values. While it was recognized that each sphere of activity, including 'religion' itself, had its place in human life, the goals of each sphere were dissimilar and their values consequently different. For values are determined by ends or goals. Tawney again:

> The theory of a hierarchy of values, embracing all human interests and activities in a system of which the apex is religion, is replaced by the conception of separate and parallel compartments, between which a due balance should be maintained, but which have no vital connexion with each other.[6]

Ironically, one of the compartments is now 'religion' itself, and even that compartment is not thought to have a vital connection with the other separate compartments. What goes into the 'religion' compartment? Ceremonial occasions and the morality of the 'private' sphere, which are as was earlier argued, the social functions still allotted to Christianity, almost fill the compartment. Christians themselves would probably expand their compartment to make it include the 'inner world', the world of the soul and the development of spiritual life, though here Christianity is certainly not alone even in Western Europe.

In the other compartments one may see how Christianity, which many years previously supplied the values for other interests and activities, is now excluded. So, for example, in the compartment of industry decisions are made according to the values of industry and not by reference to any wider system of values, let alone an ultimate one. Industry has an assumed goal – maximum profits – and consequently its values flow from this goal. All other things being equal, the 'morality' of industry is determined by this goal. Those actions

which lead to maximization of profits are 'good'. Those which impede
it are 'bad'. 'Efficiency' in particular becomes a desirable means to
greater profits. Shareholders in a public company expect management to pursue these goals. Policy towards industrial pollution and
labour relations, for example, tends to be decided according to
the profit motive and not any external moral standards.

Compartmentalization not only allows this sort of 'functionalist'
mentality to develop; it also discourages the asking of fundamental
'why' questions. If one asks an industrialist why, for example, he is
making colour televisions he will answer 'because people want to
buy them'. The meeting of a need is reckoned to be sufficient answer.
More fundamental questions are not asked because they involve
reference to other compartments, and to ultimate questions and
ultimate values, which cannot, of course, be fitted into compartments
and which can therefore be disregarded.

Education, too, is a separate compartment of life with its own
goals and values. Education is believed to be something which occurs
between five and sixteen, eighteen or twenty-one (or thereabouts)
and consists in the filling of the mind. It is thought to be an activity
with prescribed limits. A reflection of this attitude was a recent
British government report on student life, which began – 'It costs
£10,000 to train a student's mind'. A Belgian philosopher commented
about this report: 'The student is an investment in "know-how". It
is not a question of his knowing what things are, but how they are:
not of knowing the essence of things, or the substance of things, but
how to combine them.'[7]

Education is a compartment with its own goal – filling the mind –
and therefore its own value-system. What helps to fill the mind is
'good' educationally speaking; what hinders the process is bad. Each
sphere of human activity now constitutes a compartment with its
own self-consistent value-system. It should be evident that these
value-systems at least sometimes necessarily clash with Christian
thinking and moral behaviour. The Christian, firstly, is always asking why something should be done. What is its ultimate purpose? If
one asks that sort of question one cannot accept easily the decisions
of industry or education (or politics) taken with reference only to the
particular goals of those activities.

Secondly, it is far from certain that decisions taken like this actually
accord with Christian values. For example, capitalism must put
profits first in order to survive. 'Labour units' must be pruned in
order to cut costs, the environment is polluted because it would

jeopardize profitability to take the necessary preventive measures, workers are enslaved to the machines they mind and the skills needed to do their jobs are steadily reduced. These are all forms of suffering and they are all caused by subordinating the value-system prevalent in industry to the goal of profitability. It would be difficult to justify any of these accepted industrial practices by a Christian value-system.

In practice, of course, whether or not Christianity condones the necessities of capitalism is not of much interest to most businessmen since the relevance of Christianity to this and other spheres of human activity is not readily acknowledged. Christianity is supposed to confine itself to its own sphere, the 'inner world', and meet the specialized requirements of performing ceremonies and supplying morality for what we earlier called the 'private sphere'. As one commentator has brusquely put it: 'What were total life values have become part-time norms.'[8]

Amid all this adherents of the Christian faith are in a difficult position. Contemporary society expects of Christians that as Christians they fulfil only the restricted roles outlined above. And if Christians do this they are forced to lead a Jekyll and Hyde existence allowing each compartment of their lives to make its own demands, while reserving the Christian values by which they are supposed to live for spheres of activity where they are their own master, their times with their family, for example. The alternative to this is to reassert the relevance of Christian values in every sphere of life, to integrate human experience according to them. Of these two extreme positions the majority of us veer towards the first. In a pioneering study in the fifties of four Birmingham parishes R. H. T. Thompson wrote that the values of church members were drawn not from the church, but from other secular groups of which they were members. These values might be exalted by association with the church, he said, but they were values which had no necessary link with Christian revelation.[9]

Those who veer towards the alternative positions include, it seems to me, the five communities described in previous chapters. In considering why this seems to be the case and how it can happen at all it is worth looking at some theological developments which have prepared the ground.

(ii) Integration

R. H. Tawney wrote at the beginning of his *Religion and the Rise of Capitalism* (first published 1926) that

it is evident today that the line of division between the spheres of
religion and secular business . . . is shifting . . . (among all denominations) an attempt is being made to restate the practical implications of
the social ethics of the Christian faith, in a form sufficiently comprehensive to provide a standard by which to judge the collective actions
and institutions of mankind, in the sphere both of international politics
and of social organization.[10]

'Secular business' might not have been aware of it, but some
theologians were working to restate the comprehensive claims of the
Christian faith.

'The guiding theme of this', says another writer,

. . . was the recognition of the totality of God's rule and the universality
of his love. If God is really the creator, upholder and redeemer of the
world, then there can be no area of life which is outside his dominion.
This means that the almost total separation between God and the world,
church and state, Christian private morality and secular public morality
is at an end. This means taking seriously the fact that God is Lord even
in politics, that the commandments and promises of the Bible are also
valid for political action, and that Christian love is a political fact of the
first order.[11]

One influential theologian to act on this was Dietrich Bonhoeffer.
Even during the early days of his clashes with the Nazis, he was
affirming the Lordship of Christ and attacking spurious distinctions
between the religious and the profane, which underlie attempts to
restrict the dominion of Christ:

The coming of the Spirit . . . does not consist primarily in a new
religiousness, but in the proclamation of a new creative act of God. And
that means the whole of life is requisitioned. It is not for a moment a
matter of putting the religious before the profane, but of putting God's
act before both religious and profane.[12]

Eight years later, writing from prison in 1944, he was more forth-
right. 'Christ is no longer an object of religion, but something quite
different, really the Lord of the world.' And again, 'Jesus claims for
himself and the Kingdom of God the whole of human life in all its
manifestations.'[13]

This puts in theological language the claim that there is no part of
life, at present compartmentalized, which is beyond the jurisdiction
of Christian values. Nor is there any particular compartment
reserved for 'religion'. This then is one stage of recent theological
developments: there is a second which is also relevant to the growth
of groups such as these five communities. From the affirmation of
what may be in theological shorthand called 'the Lordship of Christ',

some theologians – and ordinary people too! – have gone on to affirm that Christians should adopt a distinctive critical position in society and a position which is critical because it is consistent with the gospel. Such a step has the following logic. If God is Lord of every sphere of life, then Christians must act out his word, the gospel, in every sphere of life. Many spheres of life are manifestly lived far from the influence of the gospel. Hence, if Christians are to live consistently with the gospel, they will find themselves at odds with the behaviour which is customary in many spheres of life. And this is precisely the position in which the five communities find themselves.

This further step is made by Moltmann, when he writes (in the passage quoted at the beginning of the chapter), of a new Babylonian exile for Christians from the social roles expected of them. In another passage he writes: ' "Creative discipleship" cannot consist in adaptation to, or preservation of, the existing social and judicial orders, still less can it supply religious backgrounds for a given or manufactured situation.'[14] Among non-European theologians, the voices from South Africa and both American continents have grown ever more urgent. The circumstances of open political oppression have thrown up comments such as this from the Colombian guerilla-priest Camillo Torres: 'The Roman Catholic who is not a revolutionary is in a state of mortal sin.' Or from the Brazilian Paolo Freire: 'But there are a growing number of people who, whether or not they still claim to be Christians, commit themselves to the liberation of the dominated classes,' realizing 'that it is not sufficient to give lip service to the idea that men and women are human beings if nothing is done objectively to help them experience what it means to be *persons*'.[15]

Back in Western Europe the Babylonian exile can take forms other than those that might appear to be narrowly 'political'. A 'theology of enough' showing Christians how they ought to set themselves apart from the contemporary consumer-culture, was developed by John V. Taylor, now Bishop of Winchester. Dr Taylor has identified the biblical grounds on which families and other collectives should opt out of what he calls the 'idolatry of growth'.[16]

This then is the second development in theological thinking which has prepared the ground for some of the action that goes on today in the name of Christ. These two developments together, the affirmation of the Lordship of Christ and the new Babylonian exile, show the theological context in which our five communities have seen their faith requiring of them rather more than what 'modern industrial society expects and requires of them'. They might not of course have read these particular theologians, might not even have heard of them. They might not use the same language, but their understanding of the present situation is like that of the theologians. These communities attempt to integrate the whole of their lives with one set of values, those derived from the gospels; secondly such an attempt at integration makes them different from their contemporaries. It can also make them different from those of their fellow-Christians who are forced to restrict 'total life values' to 'part-time norms'.

The word 'attempt' is used for two reasons. First one ought to avoid giving the impression that these communities have succeeded in the integration of their lives with Christian values. They have had both successes and failures. Furthermore, full integration can be carried out only by complete withdrawal from our unintegrated world, a step which is both extremely difficult and undesirable to communities whose aim is to be practical models. Such a withdrawal was not Jesus' response. Examples from the life of the five communities show how the attempt is being carried out – and in different ways.

(iii) Integration in Practice – Work

'Work' is one of the spheres which most of us assume to be outside the area of relevance of Christian values – outside the Lordship of Christ, to use the theological term. 'Work' ought then to provide an example of the communities' attempt to live under the Lordship of Christ.

Emmaus had gone furthest in the integration of its work with the rest of life. The day at this community was made up of a balanced rhythm of work and worship, which played the greatest part in the overall rhythmic pattern of life. Certain principles underlay the whole of this pattern; theirs was not a life divided into compartments. Material poverty and service of others underlay not only their life-style (what they ate, what they owned, how they spent their money) but their work, for their work of reclaiming thrown-out articles for resale or recycling was inseparable from everything else.

The other four communities did not have this degree of integration, because the way they had chosen to live did not allow it. For example, while at Emmaus everybody worked on the same job, some members in all the other communities 'went out' to work. In these cases the choice of job showed the communities' concern not to exclude their work from the overall principles by which they lived.

The choice was made according to different criteria. Members of Cinisello felt they should take jobs which would, however indirectly, further the 'workers' struggle'; members of the Laurentiuskonvent were expected not to take jobs even remotely connected with the armed services. In addition, they could not manage capitalist enterprises. There was a similar, but informal understanding at the Birmingham Community House. For certain individuals the choice became even more restricted. During the course of 1974 one member of the SCM House decided that in good conscience he could no longer go on teaching because of his dissatisfaction with the educational system. And at Greenbus there were some who held vegetarian views of a kind which would not allow them to take jobs with the two main local industries. These were a shoe factory and a sheepskin factory, both of which use animal skins in their products.

The choice of jobs was thus subject to the application of the principles by which the communities lived. In other words if an occupation was unacceptable on the community's premises, so to speak, it was unacceptable for members to practise it outside the community. 'Work' was not something to be done only in order to earn a living; it had also to be something which furthered the general aims of the community. This is an example of integration, the integration of work with the rest of life.

(iv) Integration in Practice – Economic Arrangements

Another sphere of life we commonly put in a separate compartment is that of our economic arrangements. Our economic decisions are not usually taken in accordance with distinctive Christian principles even though we may apply these to our family life. We not only maintain different standards for these different spheres, but are not aware of any relevance gospel teaching may have to the former. The five communities, on the other hand, though their arrangements differ and depend on their circumstances, consciously keep to what they understand to be the implications of Christian teaching. In all five there is a degree of common ownership of both money and goods. In Laurentiuskonvent this is full community of goods and there is nothing which is not communally owned. Though the circumstances of the other four communities do not permit this degree of common ownership their economic arrangements reflect their similar concern to make as equitable a distribution of money and goods as possible. Emmaus pays each member the same wages and gives everyone the same standard of board and lodging. Cinisello has a system of redistribution of members' salaries. Greenbus' 'Family' all contribute equally to a kitty and do not ask contributions of those who can not afford them. The SCM Birmingham House shares its consumer goods (such as they are) and also a common kitty.

Common ownership is a conscious attempt to bring day-to-day experience under the imperatives of the gospel. It is more than a series of practical arrangements. It implies that the individuals within these communities intend to overcome the attitude that money and goods are solely for the use of the family or individual who has acquired them. The consequence of this is that members of these communities manage to become less reliant on material goods. Emmaus expressed the value of this as 'living in solidarity with those who are poorest'.

The further implications of common ownership indicate how far our society expects individuals and families to 'own their own'. The attempt to live an integrated life shows here again how far this necessitates 'being different'. But common ownership has two more implications which take the contrast further. First it throws into question the need for every unit to own one of everything. This is assumed to be desirable in our society, which depends on the Smith family envying the Jones family what it owns. If the advertisers do not succeed in making the Smiths envious of the Jones then consumption cannot increase, fewer goods will be made and workers will be laid off. It is the dependence of capitalist society upon this cycle which common ownership throws into question. Communities use fewer goods among a larger number, and sometimes in addition do without those goods which society considers desirable, even necessary.

And secondly, common ownership in effect undermines the tendency, which some commentators have identified in our contemporary society, to identify ourselves not in relation to people, but to material objects; not, in other words, in terms of our relationships with others, but in terms of the objects we possess. The material (and especially the so-called 'consumer') goods we possess, actually become part of the answer to the question 'Who am I?' 'I am a house/car/colour television/washing-machine (automatic, front-loading, of course!) owner' may not be our actual words, but there can be no doubt that these objects contribute to our status and our self-esteem. We feel inadequate if we do not own these. 'Material objects rather than human beings must be called upon to testify to our inner worth' say Peter Berger and Thomas Luckmann.[17]

These same authors go on to explain this contemporary tendency as a consequence of our increased geographical and social mobility. We are so often commuting, moving house, changing jobs, visiting relatives who are no longer round the corner, not to mention taking holidays, attending meetings and so on, all in different places, that our relationships can no longer be developed to the depth of yesteryear when an individual could be almost certain of spending most of his life with the same people in the same place. Indeed we have suddenly noticed the poverty of our relationships because we can no longer take them for granted. (It should be said that these authors do not intend to make a blanket generalization, and consequently the word 'tendency' is used. There are both urban and rural areas which could be excluded.) The substitute we appear to have found for these patterns of relationships is material goods.

Those who practise common ownership are undermining this tendency in both a 'negative' and a 'positive' way. 'Negatively' they own fewer goods and hold them in common anyway. 'Positively' and correlative with this, members of communities look to each other for support and enjoy a wide network of close relationships which are relatively stable. Even if the community is not permanent, or even if the member is not permanent, he must be prepared to develop close relationships with his fellows while he is there. These will, on the whole, be different relationships from those common today.

In a community the individual or family shares his life with others with whom his relationship is not one of blood or marriage. At Laurentiuskonvent and Cinisello there were families within the community, but these had close relationships with all the other members. Likewise, unmarried people were able to develop close relationships with the families as well as with other single people.

An emphasis on personal relationships and the *quality* of these is common to nearly all communities. Mutual trust and understanding and shared objectives all depend on good personal relationships. Those communities where open tensions occurred (the SCM Birmingham House and Greenbus of these five) only emphasized the more the importance of such relationships. A true closeness demands complete openness between members, and this is not easily achieved. Sometimes encouragement is needed. One member of the Birmingham House referred to their 'honesty-sessions', which were an opportunity for members to work through rather than gloss over any hostility or disagreement between them. This practice, which Emmaus used occasionally also, occurs in many other communities and owes much to the theory of encounter group therapy. The Richmond Fellowship Community Houses have adopted it as part of their therapeutic after-care for those who have been in psychiatric care. The Blackheath Commune of 1969–1971 aired both personal problems and inter-personal tensions within the context of a weekly meeting of all members. One member said that this had helped her to learn to be honest with people while caring for them very much.[18]

Members of communities must expose themselves to each other in a way most people are able to do only with their families. Communities are, indeed, families of a kind.

(v) *Integration in Practice – The Nuclear Family*

But they are not families . . . at least not nuclear family units of Mum, Dad and the children. And it is in the differences between them and the contemporary family that the way of life of these communities sets them most obviously apart. The most striking fact about an intentional community is, after all, that although it does not have the structure of a family it has the same importance for its members. There is a certain irony associated with this. While contemporary Western man looks on the family as the Christian heartland, but does not (as we have just seen) regard work and economic arrangements as the proper sphere of Christianity, our five communities apparently regard work and economic arrangements as coming under the sway of Christianity, but question the attitude of our society towards the nuclear family. This is not because of any antagonism to the family *per se*, but rather because they do not consider that the nuclear family of the twentieth century is the institution in which the love between parents and children, and between adults, and between children, can most fruitfully grow. The single family unit *can* be, to use the language of this chapter, a barrier to an integrated life led according to the gospel. This will be explained below; but first some background.

There have been many Christian communities in previous centuries, but none which have existed to the accompaniment of the sort of criticism of the role of the nuclear family that can now be heard. This criticism has come, for example, from unconventional psychiatrists like R. D. Laing and David Cooper.[19] The ideas of these psychiatrists were popularized at the beginning of the decade by the film *Family Life* in which the sickness of a suburban girl, Janice, is shown to be the result of family pressures. Janice's family is unable to cope with her slightly unconventional behaviour. At the same time

Family Life shows how all the members of Janice's family are the victims of a society which is in constant change and makes it impossible for her family to give Janice the understanding and care she needs. It is indeed fundamental to the thought of Laing and his colleagues that the sickness or psychiatric 'disorders' of individuals can be understood only in the light of social institutions and particularly that of the family. And conversely health and psychiatric 'order' can only thus be understood. Some members in some of the five communities mentioned that they had read Laing's writings, but a greater number was aware of the ideas. The suspicion which others had of the nuclear family was the result of experience or instinct rather than of profound thought.

Christian communities in earlier days may have made criticisms which touched at a tangent the life of the family, but it was not dissatisfaction with the family unit which caused most to try something different. This was because the norm of family relationships in earlier centuries was not the nuclear family as we know it, of Mum, Dad and the children, but the 'extended' family, in which uncles, aunts and their children, and grandparents if they were still alive, formed a wider network of intimate relationships. In an essentially agricultural society the cohesive extended family met needs, gave succour, and provided mutual support to its members. (Social and economic developments interrupted this pattern occasionally but emigration to the towns from the country, or even to foreign lands, was not sufficient to alter the norm, which remained that of an extended family linked geographically and economically.)

It is only since the Industrial Revolution, and particularly in the twentieth century, that this pattern has broken up. The breaking up has been helped by the tendency to have smaller families. The single family unit of Mum, Dad and the children has tended to become separated from other parts of the family. The grandparents live alone or in a home while uncle and aunt have their own unit in another part of the country. The consequences of this have been grave.

It is now accepted,[20] for example, that the rootlessness felt by many who have moved voluntarily or been compulsorily transplanted to new housing estates on the edges of our towns and cities is due to the break-up of their former wide and supportive networks of relationships, including those of the family. Many people now notice the absence of this network. Most of those now forming themselves into intentional communities come from a generation whose experience is of the nuclear family unit. They yearn for the wider network of intimate relationships. And so, simultaneously with the decline of the extended family, there is an emphasis on the quality and quantity of the relationships which were part of that institution. Greenbus, for example, referred to the core of its group as 'the family'. In a quite explicit statement the Kingsway community, which was founded in London in the mid-sixties, has written that the establishing of Christian extended families is the greatest need.[21]

Intentional communities attempt to recreate a wider pattern of intimate relationships. Many believe the relationships of nuclear units to be inferior to those of extended units. While this may be part of the mythology which community living has evolved it is certainly part of the mythology of our society as a whole that the family with which we are familiar is a pre-eminently Christian institution. But, as Thomas Luckmann says, the real nature of the modern family is in fact 'successfully camouflaged by vocabulary derived from traditional Christian rhetoric'.[22] This 'rhetoric' includes the sentimental rendering of the story of Christ's birth, and biblical phrases such as 'Suffer the little children to come unto me', usually quoted completely out of context. But neither the circumstances of Christ's birth, nor his love of children, nor indeed his teaching on the subject of the relationship between man and God or man and man, can really be adduced in support of the twentieth-century nuclear family. They only camouflage it.

The main problem is that Christ was not familiar with our nuclear family. In his time, the unit of Mum, Dad and the children was firmly rooted in the wider network of relationships of the extended family, an institution which is still largely preserved in Mediterranean countries. Anything he says about the family (and unfortunately he says very little apart from his teaching on divorce, except to ask that ambiguous question 'Who is my mother, who are my brothers?') and about personal relationships must be seen in that light. We may well have reached the time when the family has changed so much from its form in Christ's day that we need to apply his teaching anew in an analysis of our nuclear family, to see whether what we have now enables or restricts the carrying out of Christ's teachings. This will be a painful business.

Some nuclear families are good, some bad. The same must be true of intentional communities. But why is it that the two are so often set over against each other? This is probably because intentional communities (particularly those which call themselves 'communes') are believed to oppose the sexual morality of the family. This stems

partly from the popular view of communes as the haunts of 'free-
loving hippies'. This view has been reinforced by the sensationalist
press. The shortlived commune inside 144 Piccadilly, in London,
during September 1969, for example, gave rise to a number of reports
like this one from a Sunday paper:

> Hippie thugs – the sordid truth
> Drugtaking couples making love while others look on, rule by a heavy
> mob armed with iron bars, foul language, filth and stench.
> That is the scene inside the hippies' fortress in London's Picadilly.
> These are not rumours but facts – sordid facts which will shock ordinary
> decent family loving people.[23]

The contrast is made between the commune and the family, at least
by implication. And there is, as the saying goes, no smoke without
fire. In some communes free love *is* a principle of the association or
an aim towards which the members are moving. The sensationalist
press, however, is not interested in principles, but in events and
happenings, and preferably with a photograph to supplement their
regular near-nude feature. The sensationalist press cannot print the
thinking and philosophy of communal living; it can only reduce it
to 'free love'.

Organs of propaganda against communal minorities, including
professedly Christian ones, have always exploited the possibility that
they might be operating dens of sexual licence, an accusation made
almost automatically when single men and women, and families,
choose to live together under the same roof or in an isolated settle-
ment. Some of the five communities with whom I lived said that their
neighbours had at first been suspicious about their sexual behaviour.
Of other contemporary groups the Children of God have suffered
from this sort of accusation wherever they have moved, but while
many accusations against them may be well-founded, this is not one
of them.

In the case of those Christian communities against which these
sort of accusations have been well-founded, so-called 'sexual licence'
has been a principle of the community's life. The Oneida Community,
for example, believed that free love (which they termed 'complex
marriage') was in accordance with the true teaching of the gospel.
Founded by a Congregationalist minister in New York State in the
late 1840s, this community believed that 'they were totally secure
from sin . . . that for the perfectly holy, marriage was abolished – a
woman was the bride of Christ, the bride of all the saints. Communism was to prevail among those who were holy, and this was

appropriate in sexual matters as in regard to property. Through their common life God would be glorified.'[24] Oneida based its sexual communism on the text: 'In the Resurrection, they neither marry nor are given in marriage, but are as the angels in heaven' (Matt. 22.30; Mark 12.25). Curiously enough this is the same text as that used by another group to justify their celibacy! These were the Shakers of the mid-eighteenth century.

In our five communities there was not even a watered-down version of the practice of Oneida. It is important to isolate the somewhat spectacular practice of groups like Oneida from the contemporary critiques made of the nuclear family. Generally speaking they have nothing to do with each other.

Two of the five communities included families. Two more included unsupported mothers and their children. Only Emmaus was entirely without children. It is clear that the *family* units had chosen to live differently from a nuclear family. But what about the single people? In the communities they might well be simply avoiding living on their own. They might have no particular attitude to the nuclear family. This was not in fact the case. All kinds of people in all five groups expressed varying attitudes to the nuclear family and there was a spectrum of opinion about it. Some had already refrained from a permanent twosome relationship because they wished to avoid setting up a nuclear family; others said they would avoid such a relationship in the future. Some were in favour of a permanent relationship with or without marriage, but could not conceive of this outside a communal situation. Others had an open mind as to whether the family or the community has the best environment for a permanent relationship. A final group was in respective communities for shelter and food and had no views on the subject.

This spectrum of opinion reveals widely differing ideas. But it is significant that there is in our time such a degree of openness about models for living and so intense a questioning of our chief living institution, the nuclear family. The primary scapegoat is *isolationism*. It is the isolation which our age forces upon the family which has, it is said, brought about the harmful effects we see around us. The isolation of the family unit is a barrier to the living of an integrated life. The family is both the victim of the compartmentalization of human experience, and the reinforcer of it. Isolation is both the cause and the symptom. Life in community, in the broadest sense of that word, is the recognition that we must not allow ourselves to be isolated.

Cinisello, speaking for northern Italy, puts the point in its characteristic jargon, but the meaning is clear:

> The need to overcome the feeling of isolation connected with traditional family life is not new ... Moreover an analysis of the organizational forms of our society creates a desire to discover a new way of living which can break away from the stifling atmosphere of the traditional limited family group, a typical product of a bourgeois society.[25]

The isolation of the nuclear family and the organizational forms of our society are inter-twined.

Let us be specific. Some years ago a song called 'Little Boxes', laughed at our predictability ('and they all live in little boxes . . . made of tickytacky, and they all look just the same') and our habit of boxing everything up neatly, indeed of making everything actually look like those separate compartments between which we have divided our activity. The family has actually become one of those compartments and we do not see, perhaps, the close link between the structure of society as a whole and the nature of our family life. When the pressure of work or the economic situation – two compartments of great significance in our lives – become too great, we retreat into our one refuge, the private world of our families. But our families do not see us at work – that is a totally separate world – and are incapable of understanding the pressures fully. Even if they could, they might find it hard to bear the responsibility for doing so. The family is an oasis of security for troubled individuals but can barely cope with itself.

This is one of the factors which contribute to the isolation of the family. The task of relieving the pressures brought about by modern society draws the family further in upon itself, often unconsciously. Without close relationships outside the family unit there is nobody to share the burden. There is little chance that each family unit will take responsibility for the world beyond itself. Each box wants not to need the next. If a need arises we are too tired to take responsibility anyway. And even contact with the box next door is only that of necessity. Alexis de Tocqueville wrote of nineteenth-century America words which might equally apply to twentieth-century Western Europe:

> Each of them, living apart, is a stranger to the fate of all the rest; his children and his private friends constitute to him the whole of mankind. As for the rest of his fellow citizens, he is close to them, but he does not see them; he touches them, but he does not feel them; he exists only in himself and for himself alone.[26]

The sense that we are only responsible for our own nuclear family is linked with the inability of many to bestir themselves as individuals when a call for help comes. In a spine-chilling story[27] Jim Forrest tells of a young girl called Kitty Genovese, who was stabbed to death in New York in front of blocks of flats whose inhabitants looked out from behind their curtains and did nothing. We do not have to go to New York for this sort of thing. In January 1975 a London bus conductor was stabbed to death in front of his indifferent passengers.

The isolation of families is reinforced by two other boxes, the motor car and the television, which are part of that replacement of personal relationships by material objects which was referred to above. The motor car, furthermore, transports its human contents from A to B without either personal contact with the people, or (probably) appreciation of the circumstances, met *en route*. The other box, the television, does bring the world of outside into the house and might potentially interrupt the peaceful security that we find within the family. But it doesn't. The picture of reality conveyed in news programmes and documentaries is hard to distinguish from the unreality portrayed in comedy, drama and advertising. The whole output has about it an air of unreality – a world of entertainment into which we can escape and which lulls us into inactivity. It has been suggested that the television is a major contributory factor to our inability to answer calls for help. They are no longer real. Nobody feels responsible. Detachment is universal. Isolation is reinforced.

Of the relationships within the nuclear family itself, some communards had specific criticisms. Some members at the SCM Birmingham House, for example, were unenthusiastic about what they saw as the enforced 'exclusiveness' of married couples. By this they were referring not so much to the custom that married couples have no other sexual relationships, as to the pressure to confine close relationships to that single relationship they have with each other. This exclusiveness, as has already been suggested, places too great a burden on the mutual resources of the couple and is likely to lead to the breakdown of some marriages. Within a community, it is felt, couples have other close relationships without weakening their own, and will probably enjoy a healthier relationship themselves as a result.

A related point was the uncertainty of some about all permanent twosomes. Some at Emmaus expressed the opinion that they could never be sufficiently certain to commit themselves to one person for the rest of their lives. Living communally, they argued, they gained the advantages of close relationships and mutual trust which many others enjoy within a permanent twosome relationship.

It was the effect of the nuclear family on the children within it which concerned others. Here it must be those two communities with families whose views must count for most, for they preferred communal living to remaining a nuclear family. The policy which they practised is the best expression of their attitude. In both Cinisello and Laurentiuskonvent the children were able (and indeed encouraged) to develop relationships with adults other than their parents. In neither case, moreover, was this a means of weakening the link between parents and children. From the children's point of view this opened them to the creative resources, opinions and so on of not just two adults but many. From the parents' point of view they were relieved of the crushing responsibility of being the child's single point of reference.

In addition the children grow up learning to live with few material possessions of their own, and learning to share what they have with other people. All this is achieved without enforced separation of parent and child, which is a feature of certain other communal experiments such as some of the Israeli kibbutzim, as it was also of the Oneida Community. Though there is no separation, neither is there what an English 'secular' commune has called 'the possessive stranglehold' of parents, who sometimes, in the context of a nuclear family, attempt to build identikit versions of themselves or their idealized selves. The almost inevitable result of this is an unpleasant rupture when the child realizes this. The community children may feel they are becoming identikit versions of the community's ideal, but the families at the Laurentiuskonvent, at least, may well leave the community for a while during the children's adolescence in an attempt to avoid this. It is only fair to point out that the test has not yet come for these two communities in which the oldest children are just about to enter their teens.

The nuclear family is seen to be both a part of, and a victim of, those social forces which act against the integration of an individual's life, and increase its compartmentalization. The symptom of this is the *isolation* of the family, with its narrow network of close relationships and its tendency not to take responsibility for the world beyond itself. And the result of this isolation is that too great a burden is placed on those within the family, who cannot turn to others intimately known to them for help, because they know nobody intimately, and their less immediate family is too distant. In contrast to this, the community is able to some extent to restore the wider pattern of relationships, spreading the burden of responsibility. Furthermore it hopes to bring children up more successfully and takes responsibility for outside needs which it identifies and deals with in its tasks.

(vi) Being Different

This discussion of work, economic arrangements and the nuclear family has been the means of showing how these communities attempt to integrate their lives according to one system of values. Their attitudes to work, the economic arrangements of the communities and their attempt to create the right environment for their own growth, and that of their children in some cases, are all part of their faltering attempts to live out what they understand Christianity to say today. This necessarily involves them in the creation of a different model from that on which Western society operates, now largely independently of Christian values. It necessarily involves them, in fact, in an 'exodus' from what society 'expects' of them as Christians.

The extent of the integration the communities actually achieve must vary. To begin with it would seem likely that the nearer the group is to the heartbeat of this society, with its assembly-lines, bureaucracies, and technologists, the more difficult it becomes to integrate its life. The nearer to the heartbeat one lives the more pronounced becomes the division between the compartments and the values they demand, and the more schizophrenic life becomes. But even Cinisello which by the nature of its work lived nearest to this heartbeat succeeded to some degree in overcoming the division of life into compartments which is a feature of the lives of most who work in industry and offices.

This suggests that there are factors in the structure of community living itself which make it easier to integrate one's life according to a consistent system of values. One of these factors may be that while most of us have different circles of people to whom we relate in our different activities or at least at work and at home, members of communities are more likely to live, work and play and do other activities with the same people. In their own way small communities such as villages and farmsteads have always done this. Different circles of people make different demands of us and we sometimes behave according to different value-systems depending on whom we are with. Indeed, the fact of relating to different groups of people emphasizes the division of our life into compartments. Furthermore the division between work and home is emphasized if one has to commute to work. In intentional communities life is lived with the same people and in the same place to a greater extent. In so far as this is the case it is easier to live by a consistent value-system, because members do not continually interact with different sets of people, all making different demands, nor lead two lives in different places.

Communal living makes it easier to integrate one's life, but it does not of course follow that this always happens. Community living also makes it easier to 'be different' which, as we said, is the likely consequence of an attempt at an integrated life. This is for the following reason.

Few of us can do without the continual 'confirmation' of what we believe and how we behave from those around us, particularly our intimates. If one holds what is broadly speaking a conventional view-point or if one behaves conventionally (according to the standards of those around one) then 'confirmation' comes easily. But if one does unconventional things, such as living at close quarters with men and women who are not part of the family, or hold goods in common, not to mention recycling second-hand goods for charitable purposes, or, as a middle-class person, work with working-class people, or any of the other multitude of things these five communities do, then there are probably no more than a few people around who can 'confirm' this behaviour. These are the people in the community. They can give each other the mutual support which they need to carry them through 'being different'. Making a one-man protest is very lonely; making a one-man revolution is impossible. The community structure can, therefore, not only enable what goes on inside it, but also confirm and strengthen it.

9

Older and Younger

There is one community among the five which is not a product of the particular circumstances of the sixties and early seventies which, as we saw in chapter 1, gave rise to a growth in intentional communities, mainly of younger people. The Laurentiuskonvent is in this sense the odd one out. Founded in 1959 by men who were then in their twenties it is now largely middle-aged. New members are joining but so far they have not been aged under thirty-five.

How do the younger communities differ from the Laurentiuskonvent? and do the ways in which they differ reflect anything in the younger generation as a whole?

(i) Pluralism

The first difference is this. Only the Laurentiuskonvent, the community not made up of young people, had a membership made up entirely of believing Christians, all belonging to the German Protestant Church. The other four, the communities of young people, describe themselves as Christian communities but not all their members would call themselves Christians. In all the communities, however, the leaders, and indeed a majority of members, were professing Christians.

The contrast is important. The four communities of younger people reflect the pluralism of the age. In terms of belief they are not religious ghettos; indeed they are open to others who might not have any articulated beliefs or might hold beliefs which are at variance with those of Christians. But at the same time three of these communities are able to keep up (not without problems in Cinisello and Greenbus) a recognizably Christian discipline of worship and Bible study.

A society such as ours, which has no unanimity of belief (a pluralistic society, in other words) produces the same problems in these

Christian communes as it does in (say) church youth groups. There is no dispute so long as you play table tennis; it is worship or study of the Bible which is likely to provide the sticking-point.

Likewise in the four younger communities members could quite happily be committed to a Christian life-style without being committed to the dogma which gives it justification. In chapter 4 it was shown that members of the Family at Greenbus, whatever their beliefs and attitude to worship, managed to share together in the Franciscan office.[1] In the other communes too there was disagreement on beliefs and worship. It was easier to agree on activities or courses of action as the right thing to do, even the right Christian thing to do, than to agree on a dogmatic scheme of belief. How long any understanding of Christian morality (in the broadest sense) can continue to exist without the support of the dogmatic system which gave it birth is another question.

Is this pluralism within the four younger communities reflecting something in the younger generation as a whole?

Our age is one which increasingly accepts that religious belief is a private and not a public matter. There remains (for how long?) the public status of Christianity as the 'official religion' of this country and certain others, but this does not reflect any overwhelming majority of Christian believers. It is simply not realistic to make assumptions about the religious beliefs and religious commitment of one's neighbour. We all know from our daily life that in the Western, supposedly Christian, countries we cannot assume that our neighbours will assent to any statement of Christian faith. As each new generation grows up the diverse beliefs of its parents are passed on, thereby perpetuating the pluralism. In any case, we are now more open to influence from the other great religions of the world, often brought to Western Europe by the immigrant communities in our midst. But perhaps the most important contribution to pluralism today is not the presence of any other religion at all, but of substitutes for religious belief. These include our profound, but often blind faith in the powers of science and of scientists ('They'll find a cure for it.' 'They'll stop the oil running out.' 'They'll find a way of making nuclear waste harmless.') Another substitute for religious belief is our curious attitude to many material goods, on which we have come to rely not just for comfort or convenience, but even for the formation of our identity.[2]

But what does this pluralism actually entail in the life of a young person?

Essentially, it allows him to make a *choice* of the religious beliefs with which he can make sense of his life. And where there is choice there is competition.

Religious organizations today are in competition with each other when they 'market' their wares. For the present-day young adult, however, the variety of wares has become so great that a comparison with a shopper in a supermarket is not inappropriate. On the shelves with labels marked 'Christian', independent evangelical groups vie for attention with church youth groups and other Christian groups representing every shade of belief. On another shelf are the non-Christian packages of religious belief such as Hare Krishna (or more accurately, the International Society for Krishna Consciousness), the Divine Light Mission and astrology. On yet another shelf are those 'products' concerned more with practice than with belief but which usually find their way to the 'belief' shelves – LSD, Transcendental Meditation, Black Magic and occult variations. The choice is formidable. The inquiring young adult may respond like the supermarket consumer by taking a package off the shelf and trying it. He can, after all, return to choose another brand if his first 'buy' does not give him the satisfaction it promises. More than one brand can be used at the same time. 'Brand-loyalty' is at a minimum; the packaging and marketing may be all-important.

This is part of a vicious circle. 'Religious consumerism', if we may call it this, follows from the pluralism of religious options in our society and at the same time reinforces it. But none of this could happen unless the young were in a position where they had to undertake a search, and exploration. 'Old men ought to be explorers', wrote T. S. Eliot[3] but the power of his words lies in the fact that it is not usually the old, but the young who are the explorers.

There has always been a certain special quality attached to the transition from childhood to adulthood. In some cultures the formal transition takes place within a limited time and is marked by recognized rituals. Roman young men donned what they called the *toga virilis* when they became recognized as adult; certain African tribes set their youthful members apart for a limited period while they formally lose their childish identity and gain a new adult one.[4] Our Western European society has no such recognized rituals which mark, and no recognized space of time which limits, the transition from childhood to adulthood. Instead we have 'adolescence'. This is a period in which our society expects of the child that he will become an adult. What the young adult does is lose in rebellion the childish identity he possessed and search for his new adult identity.

All young adults undertake this search to some extent. They may well be searching for a religion: they will certainly be searching for careers or jobs, and for partners. Some may also be searching for political principles and/or for a particular kind of life-style.

Not all young people in all ages, however, need to undertake a search of this kind. If a young man adopts the religious beliefs of his parents, follows the trade of his father and marries the girl down the road, he will not be psychologically footloose and engaged in this sort of search. In our society where these elements of continuity are rare, the young person has considerable searching to do to discover his or her way. This has been increasingly the case for perhaps a hundred and fifty years. This discontinuity between the generations means that the child growing to adulthood often comes to see the world differently from the way his parents see it. Tensions between parents and children (perfectly natural in all ages) are compounded by today's particular circumstances. For today, life changes so fast that parents may be trying to hand on aspects of their life, even beliefs and values, to children who have grown up in a world in which these apparently make little sense.

In today's situation two points of reference matter more to the searching young person than what his parents think or would do. One is his experience; the other is his contemporaries. Personal experience counts for a great deal. If it seems to a young person that his parents and their generation live in a different world, then what he himself has experienced will matter rather more to him than his elders' wisdom. Even if his elders' wisdom is proved right in the end, it will be proved right only by virtue of being tried and tested for himself. In this context the contemporary emphasis in many different quarters on having one's *own* religious experience is comprehensible. Different groups and individuals whose aim is to enable an individual to have his own religious experience, be that Transcendental Meditation, LSD-25 or the 'Jesus Trip', have flourished in response to eagerness for the 'real thing'.

The other point of reference in the search is that of the young person's own age-group, or peers. They can provide, or at least share, values, standards of behaviour and opinions. These are symbolized by the visible and audible links of common dress and common music.

This is to say that contemporary youth is conscious of itself as a particular group within society. And this is confirmed continually by society itself. Social institutions (including the churches) organize youth work, implying that youth has special needs. Business makes a great deal of money out of this 'peer-consciousness'. Theodore Roszak writes:

> Teen-agers alone control a stupendous amount of money and enjoy much leisure; so, inevitably, they have been turned into a self-conscious market. They have been pampered, exploited, idolized, and made almost nauseatingly much of. With the result that whatever the young have fashioned for themselves has rapidly been rendered grist for the commerical mill and cynically merchandised by assorted hucksters.[5]

In summary then, the particular quality of the transition from childhood to adulthood in Western society is a search. In this search, part of which may well be a search for religious belief, it is the young person's own experience and the thoughts and behaviour of his own age-group which are most important. Eeverybody's search is different, so are their discoveries. That is pluralism; it is also the background for the members of the four younger communities.

(ii) Impermanence

The second difference between the Laurentiuskonvent and the other four groups is that the former has permancence.

Members of the Laurentiuskonvent undertake a life commitment to each other after a 'novitiate' in which they in effect test their vocation as potential member of religious orders must. The commitment of the individual or family is permanent after that. In none of the other four groups was this permanent commitment made. Members were not bound to each other for life, or indeed by any bond except their own continuing compatibility.

Although in each of the four groups there was a nucleus of leading members who had been there since the community began, and who gave continuity to the community, other members were transient by comparison, remaining in the community for varying lengths of time. This time was longest in Cinisello which, apart from the Laurentiuskonvent, had the greatest stability of membership. The presence of families probably had something to do with this.

In the four younger communities few were sure that their search had ended. Most expected to move on when the time was right. The move might be to another community. The two leading members in the SCM House moved (separately) to new communities during late 1974. At Emmaus, Langeweg, there was an almost complete turnover of membership during 1974 though the leading members remained.

At Greenbus members changed from year to year, though some did return annually to become part of the community.

Thus the original members of the Laurentiuskonvent were prepared to make life-long vows of commitment to each other in their twenties in 1959 while none of the four more recently founded communities have been prepared to do this. Some new communities *are* still making such commitments (most notably, perhaps, the Focolare[6]) and one certainly ought not to claim that a wholesale change of attitude has taken place since the young men of the Laurentiuskonvent made their commitment to each other in 1959. But nevertheless these four communities and a large number of those communities mentioned in chapter 1 have an impermanent quality. Those who are now young are probably slow to make *any* permanent commitment, let alone to a community.

Impermanence is indeed, like pluralism, a characteristic of our time. Change is an accepted part of life. The whole ethos of our life is change. During his life a man may uproot himself from the class into which he was born and almost certainly will from the place where he was born. Society itself is in continuous and fast development, demanding of individuals that they constantly adapt. There are powerful social influences advancing impermanence, the advertising industry, for example. Goods from deodorants to vodkas are sold to us with advertisements which imply that they will change our lives. Change and dissatisfaction with what one has is indeed a necessity of the Western economic system. One hire purchase company advertised in 1974: 'Change your car for summer'.

Those who are now young expect often to change jobs, styles of clothes, religious beliefs and perhaps even partners in the coming years.[7] And the search and exploration which are the necessary consequences of pluralism themselves add to the changeful life of the young.

(iii) Informality

A third difference between the Laurentiuskonvent and the four younger communities is the nature of their respective structures. Taking, for example, their structures for decision-making we see that these are very different. While Laurentiuskonvent held absolutely regular meetings for decision-making the other four communities held meetings only sometimes, for example when major policy decisions had to be taken. More often decisions in these four would be *ad hoc* and made by whoever was best placed to make them. There were, in other words, no formal arrangements. In the Laurentius-konvent, on the other hand, community meetings were weekly and all members were expected to attend.

And necessarily the member of the Laurentiuskonvent had a different relationship to his community than a member of the other four to his community. In the Laurentiuskonvent the individual renounced the right to all his personal belongings and all his salary. Anything he owned was in effect given to him by the decision of the whole community. In the same way the Laurentiuskonvent member did not necessarily expect to practise the profession for which he or she had qualified. The nature of his or her job was decided by the community as a whole. This degree of surrender of self to the community's will did not take place in the other four communities, whose members retained certain personal belongings and, in three of them, the right to do whatever job they chose. (Emmaus is different since in joining the community the individual expresses his wish to do a particular job – 'rag-picking'.)

While Laurentiuskonvent lays emphasis on the authority of the whole community the other four do not. Authority in the latter, while it is not formally vested in any particular member, naturally devolves on to individuals. Since authority is informal it carries with it the implication that 'obedience' is voluntary and at the discretion of the individual. So it is that in the four communities each individual has great freedom to act upon his own initiative and to work with comparative independence. Part of this freedom is the freedom of belief which is necessary in the pluralistic situation of these four communities. These groups seem to reflect in their internal working the ethic of the Commune Movement (though none of them is actually a member):

> Everyone shall be free to do whatever he or she wishes, provided only that he or she does not transgress the freedom of another.[8]

Does this difference between the Laurentiuskonvent and the other communities also reflect, as the previous two did, trends in the younger generation as a whole?

While one might be able to make out a case for increased informality among younger people in dress, relationships, social behaviour, worship and other areas of life too, this does not always apply to the structures of contemporary communes of young people. The informality of our four younger groups was contrasted with the clearly defined structure of the Laurentiuskonvent. It could also be contrasted with the chain of communes run by the Children of God.

On joining a Children of God colony (as their communities are called), the new convert not only forgoes the right to any personal property but also to freedom of belief, opinion and action. This freedom is not relinquished to the general will of the community, but to the hierarchy of the organization. The authority of the hierarchy is vested in the leader of each colony, known as the 'shepherd', who is picked by the national organizers. As a result of forgoing these rights the community member's belongings are sold to add to the funds of the organization. His beliefs are fundamentalist, in accordance with those approved by the hierarchy; his opinions are derived from expositions of scripture by those in whom authority is vested, and the writings of the international leader of the Children of God, David Berg; his actions are those approved by the hierarchy for the expansion of the organization.[9] (In fairness to the Children of God, it should, be said that at the time of going to press, information was received that the decisions of the Children of God were coming to be made more and more by consensus at the colony level.) A similar authority structure to that of the Children of God can be found in another international group, the Unification Church[10] (also known as the Unified Family or the Holy Spirit Association for the Unification of World Christianity).

Both informal and 'authoritarian' groups have appeal for young people. Their attractions are completely opposite. This reflects an ambivalence in contemporary society. While the trend to informality, the questioning of authority, and the 'do your own thing' movements go on apace, others are clamouring for 'law and order', for the return of capital and corporal punishment, and government assumes ever more control. The membership of authoritarian movements of the right grows.

In the specific context of young people the change and uncertainty which is part of their life can bring a reaction. Their search ends abruptly. As Albert van den Heuvel, a leading Dutch churchman, says, 'Both the fundamentalist and the dictator will have a large following among adolescents; the result in each case is the establishment of a prison in which continuous reflection, basic to our time, is stopped.'[11]

The structures of the Children of God are hierarchical; those of the Laurentiuskonvent ensure democratic decision-making. Although both are different from our four younger groups they are just as different from each other.

In this case what is true of the four younger communities could not be said to be altogether true of the younger generation as a whole. Pluralism and impermanence were found to be reflected in wider society and this reflection provides a significant counterbalance to the previous two chapters. Those discussed the ways in which the communities stood over against Western society. In this chapter examples have emerged of ways in which these contemporary communities actually mirror developments in Western society.

(*iii*) *The Future?*

Pluralism, impermanence, informality; but the greatest of these is impermanence. Pluralistic beliefs within the community, the inevitability that some members will move on and the lack of definite structure are all features of the younger communities. And they all threaten the futures of these groups.

But does that matter? Would it matter if the communities broke up?

Such a fate might appear to some to constitute failure. But a break-up might in fact be the result of a conviction of faith that the community could not achieve anything further, given the limits of its character. This was the case with the Blackheath Commune, which existed between 1969 and 1971.[12] Like other intentional communities over the last few years this came alive when it was needed and disbanded when its members wished to attempt something else. Though Blackheath faced problems such as different levels of sensitivity to mess, dirt and so on, the unwillingness of some to be entirely frank, and saturation with needy outsiders, none of these had been insurmountable. And, significantly, there had been no unwillingness to share goods, financial arrangements, space and external activities.

Certain members had tended to take more responsibility for the community than others. This led to a strain being put upon them. A lone married couple is likely to treat a community as home with the responsibilities that that implies even if their fellows, being single people, think of it as a transitional state to which they are only temporarily committed. Then the problem of frankness, or lack of it, means that tensions can build up between members, living at such close quarters as they do, unless there is a readiness to risk oneself in talking these tensions through. This in itself can be emotionally draining. In the end it can even break up a community. The problems of both unequal responsibility and the necessity for complete frankness are of course just as much problems experienced by ordinary families.

When a community which is not primarily for the therapy of outsiders is open to anyone who comes to it in need of care, as Blackheath was (and Greenbus and Emmaus are) there can come a point at which the needy demand so much that community life cannot continue. Any community which is prepared to open its doors should also be prepared for the intense demands this makes, unless, like Emmaus, it has work on the spot to which all can contribute.

It was not any one of these problems which brought Blackheath to an end. Blackheath closed simply because it felt that it had done all it could usefully do. Its members wanted to move on to new experiences, having learnt from their experiment.

The same may well happen to the four younger communities; Laurentiuskonvent, on the other hand, is likely to last the lifetime of its members.

10

Signposts

The concluding chapter in books such as this is often an opportunity for the author to throw off his ill-disguised impartiality and advance his own opinions.

But it will probably be clear that I have not been entirely impartial in the preceding chapters. I started from a position sympathetic to those communities I was describing; and while sympathy has not, I hope, made me starry-eyed, it has certainly determined the course of the whole project.

As the research for, and writing of, this book progressed, I realized that I myself was changing. It was essential to attempt to identify in turn with each of the five communities with which I briefly lived. One cannot do that without being a different man at the end of it all. But unlike the members of those communities I was alternating that kind of life with my normal existence. I began to appreciate the force of the contrast between communal living and the life-style of the rest of us, simply because I was experiencing both ways of life.

It is this personal experience which underlies the emphasis laid in this book upon communal living as a different way of life. Others might have adopted different approaches. For example more emphasis might have been laid on the place of communities in the history of the church; or the community descriptions might have been used as the basis of a rigorously academic sociological analysis; or the descriptions might simply have been extended and the matter left there.

Instead, my own experience of the sharp contrast between the life-style and assumptions of communal living and those of Western society as a whole, led me to explore that angle and its roots in Christianity and contemporary social discontent. It seemed also important to explore more precisely the content of the contrast, and indeed, some ways in which these five communities actually reflected developments in society as a whole.

There is another point about the approach adopted in this book which ought perhaps to be specifically stated. The descriptions of the five communities are no more than cameos, pinpointing their lives at the time at which I visited them. These snatches of life cannot therefore claim to be up to date, even at the time this book was sent to the publisher. Life in some communities had changed even between my visits and publication. Membership is shifting, and new members bring new ideas. Evolution in these communities is inevitable and is probably not undesirable.

Five communities have formed the basis of this book. They are very different from one another, growing as they do from five dissimilar situations, responding as they have done in varying ways. It would have been foolish to attempt to generalize about every aspect of their lives, because, for example, what applies to the Cinisello community is not always likely to apply, say, to the Greenbus community. It would also have been false because there is no coherent communal movement. But each of these five communities was conscious of being different from its fellow members of society. They might have little contact with other communities, but of the contrast between life in communities and life elsewhere they were very aware.

This contrast is not in their imagination. An outsider coming in to them is immediately struck by the way in which the members of these communities have indeed (to return to the phrase of chapter 8) 'made an exodus' from much that is regarded as conventional social behaviour. They have adopted a structure for living which is larger and more open than most contemporary nuclear families. They have decided to take responsibility for their neighbours rather than ignore them or compete with them. They attempt to live out in their communities a life-style different in many ways from the majority one; by sharing goods and earnings and common tasks of service, by living simply so that others may simply live, by attempting, in short, to integrate *all* their lives with the teaching of the gospel.

Of necessity this sort of life also involves an exodus from the behaviour which a secular society expects of Christians. This is partly because, while society expects Christianity itself to give meaning to certain ceremonies and to legitimate certain moral stances, it does not expect Christians to have a specific attitude to social needs or to have a particular life-style.

But this, which society does not expect of Christians, is just what these communities try to have. Firstly, their attitude to social needs is one of responsibility. They may all engage in different tasks and start from varying ideological and political standpoints, but each community is committed to taking responsibility for others in our world. This is a specific sort of attitude to social needs. Even those communities which appear to withdraw from the world's hurly-burly, like Emmaus, are quietly taking responsibility for others. This begins often in the act of taking responsibility in mutual support for others nearest to them, their fellow communards. (Contrast this with the real withdrawers from responsibility such as many nuclear families caught up in the race for social advancement and more material goods. Their attitude has to be like anyone else in a race—every man for himself. The fact that the unit which is doing the racing is not an individual but a family often obscures the essential selfishness of the competitors.)

Secondly, communal living is one example of a particular sort of life-style. In the various aspects of daily life, and in differing degrees, these communities illustrate a way of living which attempts to shun the pursuit of material riches, consumer goods and social advancement. They attempt not only to share their goods and earnings, but actually to rely less on material goods for their security. They work together, where they can, at jobs which are chosen not with the sole aim of earning as much reward as possible, but rather in accordance with principles to which they subscribe.

Is it all just the self-indulgence of a deviant few who feel they have to be different? It could be said that these communes are seeking holiness and moral purity on the backs of the rest of Western society. That will no doubt express the views of some.

But I hope this book has shown that one can be more positive about the strivings of these Christian communes. They are reacting against what they feel to be the moral compromises of those around them. Their distinctiveness follows from their constructive alternatives, and necessarily sets them apart as religious and other minorities are always set apart.

But while they may be set apart ideologically and morally they are not necessarily set apart, physically. None of them has literally separated itself from the world around it. Indeed it would be possible to walk past Cinisello's block of flats or Greenbus' camp and not be aware that anything out-of-the-ordinary was afoot.

This anonymity immediately recalls the image of the leaven in the lump, the fermenting agent which, though tiny in size, affects all the flour to which it is added.

And indeed this leaven is not only fermenting away in our lump, but may be more widely relevant than one might suppose. For example, the communal model has, I believe, relevance to the network of local Christian groups in parish and congregation (and not only to *those* sorts of local groups, it need hardly be said) and to the structure of the family. Let us look at these two topics in greater detail.

Firstly, what relevance does communal living have to the mass of local groups of Christians across Western Europe? The early Christians, according to Acts, lived, if not communally, certainly at close quarters with each other. Today Christians are in a minority in Western Europe for the first time since those early centuries. Of course one *can* argue that a majority of people in Western Europe are baptized and received into membership of their institutional churches. In Scandinavia it is even the case that baptism is still seen as a kind of ceremony of initiation into state, as well as church, membership. Technically, therefore, it could be argued that Western Europe is still Christian. One still hears it said that we live in a Christian society. But those who take seriously Christ's life and claims are, as we all know instinctively, without the help of the opinion polls, not in a majority. Christianity is, as a belief system and way of living, adhered to by only a minority of Western society.

There is no doubt that the residential community model has much in its favour as a way of life for a minority grouping within a larger society which is indifferent or even sometimes hostile. The members of a community give each other mutual support, which is particularly important when one is beleaguered by indifference or hostility. The role of communities in confirming and strengthening their members was briefly explored in chapter 8. Then secondly a group of people taking on a project can often be more effective than isolated individuals doing so. Witness the activities of some of the five communities described in this book; some of the other communes briefly mentioned in chapter 1 would have shown this equally clearly.

There are additional reasons why the community might be a suitable model for the Christian minority grouping. The usual structure of the Christian community is the parish or congregation whose centre is a church building. But we seem to be seeing in the 1970s the breakdown of that structure. Lack of necessary finance to maintain this system may well be the precipitating factor. But there is a more fundamental cause than this which has not merely been shaking the foundations but actually removing them, so that even if the financial situation changed, the process of breakdown would not be stopped. This more fundamental cause is the process by which the claims of Christianity have been edged out of the centre to the very fringe of life so that for most they are at best peripheral. As the 'integrator' of the whole of a person's life Christianity is only accepted by a very limited number.[1] The structure of parishes and congregations was workable – perhaps necessary – in an age in which Christianity was the 'integrator' of everybody's life. It does not correspond to the real situation today.

The structure, however, has one vital strength which we should rescue from oblivion. In most cases the congregation is a gathering of *local* people. A parish indeed is a defined local area. The congregation is the Body of Christ in a particular place. This we must hold on to. But the Body of Christ in most places does not have the kind of distinctiveness about it which these five (and other) communities have. Its now unusual belief-system gives it minority status but its distinctiveness rarely goes any further than this unusual belief system. Kenneth Leech writes memorably of Stewart Headlam, a great Anglo-catholic of the end of the nineteenth century, that for him 'the Mass was the weekly meeting of rebels against a Mammon-worshipping social order'.[2] Unfortunately there are few today (were there really more in Headlam's time?) with this sort of understanding of the role of the Body of Christ. The Body of Christ in fact, more often than not, readily complies with 'what modern industrial society expects' of its members.[3] Its life-style hardly differs at all.

But the future may hold something different. As the parish and congregational system crumbles of its own accord, the intentional community may well, instead of being a kind of fringe unit as it is at present, become the primary local unit of Christian membership. Groups of Christians will need a closer network of relationships, greater mutual support, the encouragement to take on projects and above all strength to maintain their distinctiveness. Those needs are, as this book has tried to show, often met in a community of believers, living and working together as well as worshipping together.

In Cinisello the community is already the primary local Christian unit. Because Italian Protestants are so scattered they have never been able to afford to have a church in each place where Protestants live. Those who live in this particular Milanese suburb have no church. Their pastor has a church building elsewhere in the city but it is not a local church. The local group of which he is the leader is the Cinisello community. For the members of this community the centre of their life is not the church building but the community. They have had to do without a local church. We in the United Kingdom shall probably have to also. There is no sign in Cinisello that the lack of a church has threatened *the* church, found as it is in the shape of an intentional community. Nor does the lack of a church mean the end of the ordained ministry, though it may well make the *full-time* ministry less necessary. Cinisello, Emmaus, and Laurentiuskonvent all had ordained clergy at their centre, as do many other contemporary intentional communities, and of these only the pastor at Cinisello was what would be recognized as a full-time minister.

This possible extension of the community model emphasizes the necessity of not living with the structures of the past simply because those are what we have. The author of the Epistle to the Hebrews wrote 'Here we have no lasting city; but we seek the city which is to come.'[4] The ability to look beyond the present assumptions to the city which is to come is essential and not least in relation to the structures of the churches.

And what of the family?

The community is never, in my opinion, a substitute for marriage. The union of two people is something so absolutely basic yet full of mystery, that the different relationships between members of a community can never approach that of the marriage bond. But the community can, I believe, improve on the nuclear family, or at least show us what the nuclear family ought to be.

Firstly the unit of Mum, Dad and children can probably overcome the dangers of isolation and the stresses of contemporary society by sharing their lives to some extent at least with other families or single people. The community can to some extent play the role of the old extended families, when a greater number of people shared the responsibilities of bringing up children and looking after one another.

Secondly there is a particular inplication for women. The community *can* be (but certainly is not always) an instrument for the liberation of women. Domestic chores and the upbringing of children which sometimes become a burden when one partner (usually the woman) has to undertake most or all of them, are shared out among a greater number in most communities. Consequently the 'domestic' partner gains a desirable freedom. It is possible with a rota system involving a number of families, to share out the care of children and home among both men and women so that no one person's development is limited or even stunted by the endless round of household duties. It is also possible for both men and women to undertake other extensive commitments without in any way prejudicing the proper care and upbringing of their children.

Then there is a whole other dimension. Part of the unsatisfactory nature of the family at present is its difficulty in taking a share in caring for those for whom society has no place – in Emmaus' words 'cast-offs'. Those who were formerly often cared for within the bosom of the larger, extended family are now consigned to specialist care, if not to oblivion, in hospitals, hostels and 'homes'.

I am thinking primarily of the elderly, but also of those with terminal illnesses, some of those who have been in psychiatric institutions and some of those with drug problems, including alcoholics. Ex-prisoners form another group, but their need is perhaps rather different. Some families can, and do, give the care that people like this need, but others cannot cope. As a result there exist many institutions such as old-people's homes, half-way houses, aftercare hostels and so on which are in the circumstances absolutely vital but still no more than a second best. It cannot be very healthy to cram together people, all of whom are categorized as having the same problems, in one group in one building.

How can this situation be avoided, and how can those whom society casts off be accorded a position which restores their dignity and sense of worth, and makes use of their talents?

Again the commune model is one answer. The elderly, for example, need surroundings where they are respected for their experience and wisdom. A community can afford the elderly the opportunity they too rarely have in our youth-orientated society to do the things they are still capable of doing. In the small family unit the presence of an old person can present such difficulties for his or her children and grandchildren that the decision is eventually made that the old person should 'go into a home'. The pressures of life have become too great for them to be able to give Grandma or Grandpa the attention they need. This never happened in earlier centuries. It rarely happens today among our Indian and Pakistani immigrants who are shocked by our treatment of the elderly.

In a larger living unit, such as a community made up of a few families, it might be possible to give the elderly the care they need by sharing the burdens which proper care inevitably creates and (just as important) help the elderly to feel able to contribute to the lives of others. This was happening at the Laurentiuskonvent.

Here, then, are some of the different dimensions of these communes' relevance for us. Even if communal living is not for us all it can certainly offer *models* for more human, more Christian living. So long as a community does this it can never really be a retreat from the world, as is so often claimed. Its example is known to a greater number than its members. In certain circumstances indeed what appears to be a retreat or a withdrawal is necessary in order to start again, to build a new kind of life free as far as possible (though it can never be entirely 'pure') from the tentacles of the old.

This tension between what is seen as the old and corrupt on the one hand and the new and the pure on the other, has a certain timelessness about it. In every generation there are those who embark on a journey away from the given and the obvious (who does not in their own small way?). The paradox is that those who have made their exodus still have influence inside the land they have been journeying away from. So it has been with monks and nuns and so it is now with these communes.

And there is another paradox about all this. Those on the journey never really build an entirely new life, never really become free of the tentacles of the old. But perhaps that is the meaning of being in the world, but not of it.

NOTES

1. Christian Communes

1. Acts 4.32–35, cf. 2.44–46. All biblical quotations are from the Revised Standard Version.

2. See Alan Maycock, *Nicholas Ferrar of Little Gidding*, 1938.

3. Quoted by Andrew Rigby, *Alternative Realities*, Routledge and Kegan Paul 1974, p. 20.

4. Quoted from a letter from Winstanley to Thomas Fairfax in 1649 by R. H. Tawney, *Religion and the Rise of Capitalism*, Penguin Books 1938, p. 254; originally published by John Murray 1926.

5. See Aylmer Maude, *A Peculiar People: The Doukhobors*, Grant Richards 1904.

6. For the Hutterites, see Bryan Wilson, *Religious Sects*, Weidenfeld and Nicolson 1970.

7. On the Anglican monastic revival see A. M. Allchin, *The Silent Rebellion*, SCM Press 1958.

8. See chapter 7, note 4.

9. For the Focolare see *The Catholic Herald*, 13 March 1970; *The Tablet*, 13 May 1972; *Frontier*, November 1972.

10. Andrew Rigby, op. cit., p. 4: Also Rigby, *Communes in Britain*, Routledge and Kegan Paul 1974, p. 4.

11. *The New York Times* 17 December 1970. William Hedgepeth and Dennis Stock, *The Alternative*, Collier Macmillan, New York 1970, p. 23.

12. For a personal account of the events of 1968 and the philosophy behind them see D. and G. Cohn-Bendit; *Obsolete Communism, the Left Wing Alternative*, Penguin Books 1969.

13. This will sound bald; but at least in so far as Christian communes are concerned this will be argued in greater detail in later chapters.

14. See Andrew Rigby, *Alternative Realities* and *Communes in Britain*.

15. See Andrew Rigby, opp. cit.; also *Community 9* for a personal account by the leader of the Kingsway community, David Horn.

16. Tony Hodgson, in *Christian Aid News*, Nov./Dec. 1974, p. 7. See also his article in *Community* (ed. David Clark, Westhill College, Birmingham 29), 8, and Michael de-la-Noy in *The Guardian*, 8 July 1974.

17. See Geoffrey Corry, *Jesus Bubble or Jesus Revolution*, BBC Youth Department (10 Eaton Gate, London SW1) 1973; *Search for Peace*, Christian Journals, Belfast.

18. See Alf McCreary, *Corrymeela*, Ray Davey (Director of Corrymeela), 'Corrymeela—Open to Hope', *Risk* (World Council of Churches, Geneva), 10, no. 1, 1974.

19. See John J. Vincent, *The Jesus Thing*, Epworth 1973, Pt 4.

20. See on Blackheath, chapter 9, pp. 104–5 below; *Peace News* (8 Elm Avenue, Nottingham), 1855, 28 January 1972; *Catonsville Roadrunner* (128 Bethnal Green Rd, London E2), 26; *Community*, 1; and Andrew Rigby,

Alternative Realities, pp. 122–4. On Newhaven see *Eclectics* (Journal of the Scottish SCM), no. 1, October 1971, and Andrew Rigby, *Communes in Britain*, ch. 2.

2. The Emmaus Community, Langeweg, Netherlands

1. Rudolf de Jong, *Provos and Kabouters*, Friends of Malatesta, Buffalo, New York, p. 15.
2. A recent discussion of the situation of the Dutch churches can be found in 'Demythologizing the Dutch', *Risk*, 8, no. 2, 1972. See also *Catonsville Roadrunner*, 41, and the author's *What is the Meaning of Faith in each Situation?*, on Holland, BCC Youth Unit, 1974.
3. For the early history of the Emmaus communities see Boris Simon, *Abbé Pierre and the Rag-pickers*, London 1955.
4. See p. 70 above.
5. See ch. 7, p. 12.
6. 69 and note *Catonsville Roadrunner*, 43.

3. The Laurentiuskonvent, West Germany

1. Quoted by Heinz Zahrnt, *The Question of God—Protestant Theology in the Twentieth Century*, Collins 1969.
2. Life at Finkenwalde is described in Bonhoeffer's own words in *Life Together*, SCM Press 1954. His writings during the Finkenwalde period (1935–1937) are available in *The Way to Freedom*, Fontana 1966.
3. From the constitution of the Laurentiuskonvent.
4. The Hebrew word *Shalom* is usually translated 'peace' but the English word barely conveys the depth of the original. *Shalom* is wishful, as well as descriptive, and expresses the aspirations of the Jewish people of the Old Testament for righteousness and justice under God's law.

4. The Greenbus Community, Glastonbury

1. A recent account of the Glastonbury legends is Geoffrey Ashe, *King Arthur's Avalon*, Fontana 1973.
2. Although Timbuktoo is probably an almost single-minded Moslem city, I think the meaning of this remark is clear. On Glastonbury beliefs see Kenneth Leech, *Youthquake*, Sheldon Press 1973, pp. 104–7. An in-depth study of this fascinating topic is to be found in an (unpublished) religious studies dissertation submitted to Bristol University by Irving Hexham, *Some Aspects of the Contemporary Search for an Alternative Society*, 1971.
3. See *Torc*, a Glastonbury magazine published from Longacre, Parbrook, Glastonbury, especially issue 10.
4. For Taizé, see chapter 7, p. 69 and note.
5. For this kind of religious pluralism, see chapter 9. The Divine light Mission is a syncretistic religion, Indian in origin, whose leading figure, Guru Maharaj Ji, lays claim to Messianic qualities.
6. The process of a group taking on in reality the picture which outsiders, particularly hostile outsiders, form of it, is described in connection with the end-of-the-sixties drug subculture in Notting Hill, London, by J. Young in S. Cohen (ed.), *Images of Deviance*, Penguin Books 1970.

7. For the difficulties arising from openness see chapter 9, p. 105.

8. See chapter 7, p. 69 and note.

9. Ley-lines are 'lines of energy or force which form a grid network all over the world . . . what the nature of this energy is does not seem clear . . . what is certain is that where ley-lines meet, a power-point is created'. Hexham, op. cit., p. 25.

10. See this chapter page 35.

11. To put it in astrological terms some believe that the universe is experiencing a planetary readjustment which will herald a New Age, which they call the Age of Aquarius. Such an adjustment is said to have happened previously around the birth of Christ when the Age of Pisces began. In Glastonbury Aquarian beliefs are linked to those figures most significant in the Glastonbury spectrum of legend and myth, Arthur, Joseph and Gandalf of Tolkien's *Lord of the Rings*.

5. The Cinisello Community, Milan, Italy

Uncredited quotations in the text are from my conversations with members of the Cinisello commune, or from a document written by themselves and published by the World Student Christian Federation, April 1974, entitled *Our Experiment in Cinisello* and available from 37 Quai Wilson, Geneva.

1. The work of these Catholic communities has been well documented. For a recent account see *Communita del L'Isolotto—Liberarsi e Liberare*, Nistri-Lischi, Pisa 1973. For documentation on the development and difficulties of these communities see the publications of IDOC, via S. Maria del Anima 30, 00186 Rome.

2. *Gioventu Evangelica 27*, via Giuseppe Mantellini 22/A, 00179 Rome.

3. The document of which this is a summary is reprinted in full in English in *What is the Meaning of Faith in Each Situation?*, on Italy, published by the BCC Youth Unit, 1973.

4. *Letter to a Teacher*, published by Penguin Books here in 1971.

5. *Gioventu Evangelica 27*, p. 12. *Soledad Brother*, Penguin Books 1971, is a collection of letters from the author in prison in California. Jackson was serving a sentence for the murder of a prison guard and was killed in an attempted jail-break in 1971.

6. See, for instance, the work of Paulo Freire, especially *Pedagogy of the Oppressed*, Penguin Books 1972 and of Ivan Illich, especially *Deschooling Society*, Penguin 1973. An interesting collection of articles on this and related subjects can be found in *To Free the Spirit*, SCM of Great Britain and Ireland, 1973. Publications of the SCM including their journal, *Movement*, are available from Wick Court, Wick, Bristol.

6. Student Christian Movement Community House, Birmingham

1. See chapter 1, note 20.

2. See below p. 61.

3. *Communiques 8*, August/September 1973.

4. On the subject of permanence see chapter 9, pp. 100–1.

5. Cinisello also experienced this difficulty; see chapter 5, p. 52.

7. Christian Radicalism

1. Charles Sorley, *Marlborough and other poems*, CUP 1922, Poem XV.
2. The literature on this is ever-increasing. See, for a theological standpoint, Gustavo Gutierrez, *Theology of Liberation*, SCM Press 1974; Basil Moore (ed.), *Black Theology, the South African Voice*, Hurst 1974; 'Incommunication', *Risk*, 9, no. 2, 1973. For descriptive accounts see 'Priests for the People', *New Internationalist* (High Street, Benson, Oxon), Dec. 1973; *Catonsville Roadrunner*, 49; *Movement* 12.
3. For the Society of the Sacred Mission and the Community of the Resurrection see chapter 1, p. 3.
4. Much has been written about Taizé. For an account of the community itself see Peter Moore's *Tomorrow is Too Late*, Mowbrays 1970; Geoffrey Moorhouse, *Against All Reason*, Penguin 1972, chapter 1. For comment on the youthful invasion of the community see *Movement* 16 and 18, 1974 and my article in *Community*, 10.
5. See chapter 4, pp. 35–6.
6. See chapter 1, pp. 4–6.
7. Alan Richardson, *A Theological Word-Book of the Bible*, SCM Press 1957, p. 119.
8. Jürgen Moltmann, *Theology of Hope*, SCM Press 1967, p. 84.
9. The Commune Movement, *A Federal Society Based on the Free Commune*.

8. A New Exodus

1. Jürgen Moltmann, *Theology of Hope*, p. 324.
2. Peter Berger, *The Social Reality of Religion*, Penguin Books 1973, pp. 133f.
3. The *cultus publicus* comparison is Moltmann's, op. cit., p. 306.
4. R. H. Tawney, *Religion and the Rise of Capitalism*, Penguin Books 1938, pp. 272–3.
5. Ibid. pp. 19–20.
6. Ibid. p. 22.
7. Cornelius van Peursen in 'Man and Reality—The History of Human Thought', *The Student World*, lvi 1963, No. 1 (WSCF).
8. Thomas Luckmann, *The Invisible Religion*, Collier Macmillan 1967, p. 39.
9. R. H. T. Thompson, *The Church's Understanding of Itself*, SCM Press 1957, ch. 8.
10. R. H. Tawney, op. cit., pp. 18–19.
11. Heinz Zahrnt, *The Question of God*, Collins, 1969, p. 173.
12. Dietrich Bonhoeffer, *The Way to Freedom*, Fontana 1972, p. 47.
13. Dietrich Bonhoeffer, *Letters and Papers from Prison*, enlarged edition, SCM Press 1971. Letters to Bethge, 30 April 1944, p. 281 and 30 June 1944, p. 342.
14. Moltmann, op. cit., p. 334.
15. Paolo Freire, 'Education, Liberation and the Church', *Risk*, 9, no. 2, 1973 and *Movement* 10, his emphasis.
16. John V. Taylor, *Enough is Enough*, SCM Press 1975.

17. Peter Berger and Thomas Luckmann, *European Journal of Sociology*, Vol. 5, 1964, p. 339.

18. See chapter 1, note 20.

19. See for example, R. D. Laing and A. Esterson, *Sanity, Madness and the Family*, Penguin Books 1970; David Cooper, *The Death of the Family*, Penguin 1972.

20. See for example, P. Willmott and M. Young, *Family and Kinship in East London*, Penguin Books 1969.

21. *Catonsville Roadrunner*, 26.

22. Luckmann, op. cit., p. 113.

23. *The People* 21 September 1969, quoted in S. Cohen (ed.), *Images of Deviance*, Penguin Books 1971.

24. Bryan Wilson, *Religious Sects*, Wiedenfeld and Nicolson 1970, p. 183.

25. Toti Bouchard, *Our Experiment at Cinisello*, WSCF 1974.

26. *Democracy in America* (1948), quoted by Moltmann, op. cit., p. 319.

27. In Alistair Kee (ed.), *Seeds of Liberation*, SCM Press 1973, pp. 30f.

9. *Older and Younger*

1. See chapter 4, pp. 35–7.

2. See chapter 8, pp. 84–5.

3. T. S. Eliot, 'East Coker', *Four Quartets*, Faber 1944.

4. See e.g. V. W. Turner, *The Ritual Process*, Routledge and Kegan Paul 1969. (On the Ndembu tribe in Zambia.)

5. Theodore Roszak, *The Making of a Counter-Culture*, Faber 1971 edition, p. 27.

6. See chapter 1, p. 4 and note.

7. See chapter 6, p. 58.

8. The Commune Movement, *A Federal Society Based on the Free Commune*.

9. For the Children of God see Enroth, Ericson and Peters, *The Story of the Jesus People*, Paternoster 1972; Geoffrey Corry, *Jesus Bubble or Jesus Revolution*, BCC 1973. Corry's work includes a useful bibliography.

10. For the Unification Church see *Crusade*, September 1974; *The Guardian*, 20 May 1975.

11. Albert van den Heuvel (ed.), *The New Creation and the New Generation*, Friendship Press, New York, 1965, p. 9.

12. See chapter 1, note 20.

10. *Signposts*

1. See chapter 8.

2. *The Times*, 18 January 1975.

3. See chapter 8, pp. 79–82.

4. Hebrews 13.13.

INDEX